AF553892

NGO Accountability
Issues and Challenges

NGO Accountability
Issues and Challenges

A.K. Srivastava

Mahaveer & Sons
(Publishers & Distributors)
New Delhi–110002

Edition 2015

ISBN-81-8377-307-2

Published by
MAHAVEER & SONS
3072/28, First Floor, Gola Market, Darya Ganj,
New Delhi–110002

Rs. 925/-

PRINTED IN INDIA

Published by Sh. Mukul Sharma for Mahaveer & Sons, 3072/28, First Floor, Gola Market, Darya Ganj, New Delhi–110002, Printed at Nav Prabhat Printing Press, Delhi.

Contents

Preface

Accountability at least points at a correspondence between actions and objectives that have been defined and agreed on. We refrain from defining accountability very tightly at the outset of this book, as its intent is to unfold a series of different angles, perceptions or conditions that may influence or determine whether or not an NGO is considered accountable. Although it may be grounded in legal obligations, accountability is a normative and socially constructed concept and it always requires interpretation of particular facts, circumstances, action or inaction. Much of the heat in debates on NGO accountability comes from those who believe that they are more entitled than others to establish such interpretations.

The literature on NGO accountability features a common thread, which is that internationally active NGOs should be subject to oversight and restraints by accountability holders. When a lens of democratic accountability is placed over NGOs, they can appear to be unaccountable because they are not publicly elected and because of the non-existence of a global public for ongoing validation of NGO actions.

Moreover, the restraints against abuse-fiscal, reputational and legal constraints-may not operate very well for some NGOs. The potential abuses include violating national laws, making false claims that tarnish the reputations of others, engaging in activities that abridge human rights, wasting financial contributions and misapprehending the public interest. In answering, one should start with the individual. What accountability for an individual's actions is expected? We expect the individual to be accountable to her conscience, to her family, to whatever deity she recognizes, to the laws of the governments that have jurisdiction over her, to entities with which she has entered contractual relations (such as employers), and generally to those to whom she has made a commitment. This is an extensive range of accountability, but hardly seems all-encompassing in the sense that an individual is to be accountable to all humans for all of her thoughts and deeds. In other words, my claim is that on a day-to-day basis, the individual engages in many acts of volition that are an exercise of her autonomy and for which no accountability is expected.

Such retaliation against private persons through joint governmental action is not a new development, as multilateral legislation against dangerous organizations began with the Protocol of 1904 against the Anarchist Movement. Mundane illegal activity in NGOs can incur accountability under domestic law. An association committing criminal acts such as financial disruptions or eco-terrorism may be prosecuted (Crimm, 2004). Associations and their employees may also be liable under domestic law for potential torts such as negligence or defamation, and for violations of tax and corporate governance requirements.

This book compiles well-researched articles on different aspects of NGO Accountability with special emphasis on the role of NGOs, contributed by leaned academics from different universities and institutions.

—*Editor*

1

Introduction

Accountability at least points at a correspondence between actions and objectives that have been defined and agreed on. We refrain from defining accountability very tightly at the outset of this book, as its intent is to unfold a series of different angles, perceptions or conditions that may influence or determine whether or not an NGO is considered accountable. Although it may be grounded in legal obligations, accountability is a normative and socially constructed concept and it always requires interpretation of particular facts, circumstances, action or inaction. Much of the heat in debates on NGO accountability comes from those who believe that they are more entitled than others to establish such interpretations.

Over the past 25 years, perceptions of NGO accountability began as a byproduct of the prevailing paradigm regarding the role of NGOs in development. Changes in the development paradigm have produced a corresponding shift in emphasis in NGO accountability discussions. Today, debates regarding NGO accountability are embedded in multiple discourses around development, security, globalization and global governance. From a by-product of better performance management in the 1980s, accountability has become a hard issue at the centre of NGOs' political and organizational profile. Below, we present a short history of NGO accountability by means of an evolving set of syllogisms that outline the prevailing perception of NGO roles, roughly in the last 25 years.

The first syllogism: Complementing government (1980-1989)

- Governments are not good at delivering public services.
- NGOs are closer to the public.
- NGOs are good at delivering public services.

Perceptions of NGO accountability focused on financial accountability, organizational capacity, efficiency and performance delivery. In this era, privatization of major sectors of a national economy was a standard approach to development. Governments were seen to be part of the problem, market liberalization was understood to be the best way to achieve economic growth and structural adjustment was the dominant methodology for restructuring relations between the state and the market. The fashionable development paradigm was to rely on markets as much as possible, to actively downsize the state and to switch social service delivery to NGOs. NGOs were considered superior to the state delivery system because NGOs were private forces and had a reputation for reaching the very poor. The capacity, however, of NGOs to deliver large-scale services was in question (Gordon Drabek, 1987).

'One of the fundamental reasons that NGOs have received so much attention of late is that they are perceived to be able to do something that national governments cannot or will not do', wrote the editor of World

Development in a special issue that provided a state-of-the-art overview of the debate on NGOs and development at the time (Gordon Drabek, 1987). After 20 years of development assistance provided by governments and multilateral agencies, the poor were not benefiting. The blame for entrenched poverty was placed squarely on the shoulders of developing country governments and justified through arguments that governments were too big and not efficient, or were corrupt. Aid and other financial resources were shifted away from government agencies to NGOs.

NGOs claimed a bigger portion of the assistance cake, and in so doing shifted from organizations focused on charity and emergency into carriers of people-centred sustainable development. It is striking how in the same issue of World Development, there is virtually no discussion of NGO accountability other than financial accountability. The focus is on how NGOs can improve their evaluation mechanisms and deliver more by 'scaling-up' the impact of their activities. Only Tim Broadhead raises the question whether NGO accountability can solely be to the sources of their funding, 'as presently is the case' or also to their partners (for Northern NGOs), or to their base (for Southern NGOs) (Broadhead, 1987).

The second syllogism: The rise of civil society (1989-1995)

- Civil society is necessary for democracy.
- NGOs are civil society.
- NGOs are good for democratic development.

Perceptions of NGO accountability focused on quality of internal governance and the formalization of organizational intent and behaviour (codes of conduct and mission statements). The second syllogism marks the first shift to a new paradigm, when NGO accountability began to be informed by questions of democracy and governance. For a short period, the fall of the Berlin Wall led many to believe that the age of democracy had begun, that civil society was critical to democracy and NGOs defined civil society. Even the crushing of the student revolt in Tiananmen Square was seen as an important signal of the 'thirst for democracy...ready to flare up again when the moment is right' (Clark, 1991).

Improving the capacity of NGOs to undertake new responsibilities as harbingers of democracy became the dominant discourse on NGO management during this period (Aspen Institute, 1997). Dissenters were already hinting at the next paradigm shift through debates about scaling up impact or deepening the quality of the interventions and ensuing civic relations (Edwards and Hulme, 1995). Perceptions of NGO accountability focused on the quality of internal governance and the formalization of organizational intent and behaviour.

The third syllogism: The rise of good governance (1995-2002)

1 Good governance is necessary for development.

2 NGOs are not different from other organizations in civil society.

3 NGOs need to apply principles of good governance.

Perception of NGO accountability focused on legitimacy and establishing selfregulation or independent accreditation mechanisms. The next period saw the gradual shift of the debate away from capacity building discussions and toward debates on the role of NGOs and civil society. In 1995, with the continued clear-failures of the prevailing development model (the so-called 'Washington Consensus' built on structural adjustment), a new development imperative-good governance-began to appear. NGOs became embedded in the sweep for good governance as they were seen as agents of development, and needing to respond better to the public (World Bank, 2006). This half-decade also sparked a revolt against the rules of development, most famously in Seattle. The great globalization debates began to eclipse the development paradigms and changed the frame within which the NGO accountability discourse took place. NGOs as a phenomenon and the role of NGOs in globalization and development began to be debated among social scientists, advocates of economic liberalization and globalization and Southern governments. NGOs became fashionable foils for globalization.

This period marked a more heated discourse on NGO accountability. NGOs responded with independent accreditation mechanisms and self-regulation through federations and associations.

The fourth syllogism: The return of state supremacy (2002 onwards)

1 Government is essential to ensure safety and development.

2 NGOs' influence is not in proportion to their credentials.

3 NGOs need to be kept in check by legitimate government frameworks.

Perception of NGO accountability focused on screening credibility and promoting external (state) control. From 2001 through to today, the discourse on NGO accountability has two prominent strands. The first reflects greater themes in the development and globalization discourses. The return of state centricity or supremacy is one clear trend. Some states feel that they have ceded far too much authority to NGOs and other private agents. The US government, for example, has recently announced a new policy requiring all aid from the US to be clearly marked as American, regardless of how or where it is distributed (InterAction, 2003).

Similar clear responsibilities to state interests are noted in myriad NGO laws, now on the increase at national levels worldwide. The perception of NGO accountability in this view is focused on screening credibility and promoting external (state) control (Manheim, 2003).

Even the World Bank has recently declared that states have a central role to play in development, which represents a complete shift from the 1980s development paradigm (Perry et al, 2006). The focus on terrorism among states is in part driving this new crackdown. Azerbaijan and Georgia, for example, have new laws governing NGOs that they have put into place as a response to the war on terror (Zullo, 2003).

The fifth syllogism: A rights-based approach (2002 onwards)

1 There is no democratic global governance supporting universal human rights.

2 NGOs assert and solidify human rights in different political arenas and regardless of the state of governance.

3 NGOs contribute to democratic governance by articulating public policy needs and practicing solutions resolving public needs.

Perception of NGO accountability focused on balancing

multiple responsibilities to different constituencies or stakeholders, using a variety of mechanisms, servicing accreditation rather than regulation. A competing fifth syllogism is also on the rise, based on principles of human rights and supported by the apparent differences of public trust in different institutions.

The Edelman Public Relation Firm, for example, launched the 5th Barometer of Trust in 2004, stating: 'Why did we start this process five years ago? We had seen the Battle of Seattle and we started to see tremendous divergence between attitudes in Europe and the United States towards the NGO sector. That's the beginning of it'. (Edelman, 2005). Edelman's Barometer of Trust has consistently ranked NGOs as one of the most trusted forms of organizations, ranking above corporations, but also above governments, churches, the media and other authorities. This public trend of trust toward NGOs competes with the rise of state supremacy and the trend towards greater control over NGOs. Apparently, the global public (at least those bits that have been surveyed) believe that NGOs generally contribute to the public good.

Over the past five years, Edelman (2005) has found that the publics surveyed believe NGOs were the closest organizational form to their own personal social networks and offered more reliable information than leaders, experts, the media, governments and corporations. The public expectation of NGO accountability, we would posit, relates to the missions and services provided to beneficiaries. It may be far more sophisticated than the command and control mechanisms that governments and corporations are seeking from NGOs. A rights-based approach to NGO accountability could service this public expectation.

INTRODUCTION TO NGO

Non-governmental organization (NGO) is a term that has become widely accepted as referring to a legally constituted, non-governmental organization created by natural or legal persons with no participation or representation of any government. In the cases in which NGOs are funded totally or partially by governments, the NGO maintains its non-governmental status and excludes government representatives from membership in the organization. Unlike the term *intergovernmental organization*, "non-governmental organization" is a term in general use but is not a legal definition. In many jurisdictions these types of organization are defined as "civil society organizations" or referred to by other names.

The number of internationally operating NGOs is estimated at 40,000. National numbers are even higher: Russia has 277,000 NGOs. India is estimated to have between 1 million and 2 million NGOs.

History of NGO

International non-governmental organizations have a history dating back to at least 1839. Rotary, later Rotary International, was founded in 1904. It has been estimated that by 1914 there were 1083 NGOs. International NGOs were important in the anti-slavery movement and the movement for women's suffrage, and reached a peak at the time of the World Disarmament Conference. However, the phrase "non-governmental organization" only came into popular use with the establishment of the United Nations Organization in of the United Nations Charter for a consultative role for organizations which are neither governments nor member states—see Consultative Status. The definition of "international NGO" (INGO) is first given in resolution 288 (X) of ECOSOC on February 27, 1950: it is defined as "any international organization that is not founded by an international treaty".

The vital role of NGOs and other "major groups" in sustainable development was recognized, leading to intense arrangements for a consultative relationship between the United Nations and non-governmental organizations. Rapid development of the non-governmental sector occurred in western countries as a result of the processes of restructurization of the welfare state. Further globalization of that process occurred after the fall of the communist system and was an important part of the Washington consensus.

Globalization during the 20th century gave rise to the importance of NGOs. Many problems could not be solved within a nation. International treaties and international organizations such as the World Trade Organization were perceived as being too centred on the interests of capitalist enterprises. Some argued that in an attempt to counterbalance this trend, NGOs have developed to emphasize humanitarian issues, developmental aid and sustainable development. A prominent example of this is the World Social Forum which is a rival convention to the World Economic Forum held annually in January in Davos, Switzerland.

The fifth World Social Forum in Porto Alegre, Brazil, in January 2005 was attended by representatives from more than 1,000 NGOs. Some have argued that in forums like these, NGOs take the place of what should belong to popular movements of the poor. Others argue that NGOs are often imperialist in nature, that they sometimes operate in a racialized manner in dominant countries, and that they fulfil a similar function to that of the clergy during the high colonial era. The philosopher Peter Hallward argues that they are an aristocratic form of politics. However, this philosophy would suggest that organizations of indigenous peoples are not represented, which is untrue. Whatever the case, NGO transnational networking is now extensive.

NGOs and its Types

Apart from "NGO", often alternative terms are used as for example: independent sector, volunteer sector, civil society, grassroots organizations, transnational social movement organizations, private voluntary organizations, self-help organizations and non-state actors (NSA's). Non-governmental organizations are a heterogeneous group. A long list of acronyms has developed around the term "NGO". These include:

- BINGO is short for business-oriented international NGO, or big international NGO;
- CSO, short for civil society organization;
- DONGO: Donor Organized NGO;
- ENGO: short for environmental NGO, such as Global 2000;
- GONGOs are government-operated NGOs, which may have been set up by governments to look like NGOs in order to qualify for outside aid or promote the interests of the government in question;
- INGO stands for international NGO; Education charter international is an international NGO
- QUANGOs are quasi-autonomous non-governmental organizations, such as the International Organization for Standardization (ISO). (The ISO is actually not purely an NGO, since its membership is by nation, and each nation is represented by what the ISO Council determines to be the 'most broadly representative' standardization body of a nation. That body might itself be a nongovernmental organization; for example,

the United States is represented in ISO by the American National Standards Institute, which is independent of the federal government. However, other countries can be represented by national governmental agencies; this is the trend in Europe.)

- TANGO: short for technical assistance NGO;
- GSO: Grassroots Support Organization
- MANGO: short for market advocacy NGO.

Classifications of NGOs

There are also numerous classifications of NGOs. The typology the World Bank uses divides them into Operational and Advocacy: The primary purpose of an operational NGO is the design and implementation of development-related projects. One frequently used categorization is the division into *relief-oriented* versus *development-oriented* organizations; they can also be classified according to whether they stress service delivery or participation; or whether they are religious or secular; and whether they are more public or private-oriented. Operational NGOs can be community-based, national or international.

The primary purpose of an Advocacy NGO is to defend or promote a specific cause. As opposed to operational project management, these organizations typically try to raise awareness, acceptance and knowledge by lobbying, press work and activist events. USAID refers to NGOs as *private voluntary organisations*. However many scholars have argued that this definition is highly problematic as many NGOs are in fact state and corporate funded and managed projects with professional staff. Furthermore it has often been argued that USAID is in fact a key arm of American imperialism and that it sets up and supports NGOs in order to further imperial agendas.

NGOs exist for a variety of reasons, usually to further the political or social goals of their members or funders. Examples include improving the state of the natural environment, encouraging the observance of human rights, improving the welfare of the disadvantaged, or representing a corporate agenda. However, there are a huge number of such organizations and their goals cover a broad range of political and philosophical positions. This can also easily be applied to private schools and athletic organizations.

Methods of NGOs

NGOs vary in their methods. Some act primarily as lobbyists, while others primarily conduct programs and activities. For instance, an NGO such as Oxfam, concerned with poverty alleviation, might provide needy people with the equipment and skills to find food and clean drinking water, whereas an NGO like the FFDA helps through investigation and documentation of human rights violations and provides legal assistance to victims of human rights abuses. Others, such as Afghanistan Information Management Services, provide specialized technical products and services to support development activities implemented on the ground by other organizations.

NGO and Public Relations

Non-governmental organizations need healthy relationships with the public to meet their goals. Foundations and charities use sophisticated public relations campaigns to raise funds and employ standard lobbying techniques with governments. Interest groups may be of political importance because of their ability to influence social and political outcomes.

NGOs and Consulting

Many international NGOs have a consultative status

with United Nations agencies relevant to their area of work. As an example, the Third World Network has a consultative status with the UN Conference on Trade and Development (UNCTAD) and the UN Economic and Social Council (ECOSOC). While in 1946, only 41 NGOs had consultative status with the ECOSOC, by 2003 this number had risen to 3,550.

Project Management

There is an increasing awareness that management techniques are crucial to project success in non-governmental organizations. Generally, non-governmental organizations that are private have either a community or environmental focus. They address varieties of issues such as religion, emergency aid, or humanitarian affairs. They mobilize public support and voluntary contributions for aid; they often have strong links with community groups in developing countries, and they often work in areas where government-to-government aid is not possible. NGOs are accepted as a part of the international relations landscape, and while they influence national and multilateral policy-making, increasingly they are more directly involved in local action.

Not all people working for non-governmental organizations are volunteers. The reasons people volunteer are not necessarily purely altruistic, and can provide immediate benefits for themselves as well as those they serve, including skills, experience, and contacts. There is some dispute as to whether expatriates should be sent to developing countries. Frequently this type of personnel is employed to satisfy a donor who wants to see the supported project managed by someone from an industrialized country. However, the expertise these employees or volunteers may have can be counterbalanced by a number of factors: the cost of foreigners is typically higher, they have no grassroot connections in the country they are sent to, and local expertise is often undervalued.

The NGO sector is an important employer in terms of numbers. For example, by the end of 1995, CONCERN worldwide, an international Northern NGO working against poverty, employed 174 expatriates and just over 5,000 national staff working in ten developing countries in Africa and Asia, and in Haiti.

Funding

Large NGOs may have annual budgets in the hundreds of millions or billions of dollars. For instance, the budget of the American Association of Retired Persons (AARP) was over US$540 million in 1999. Funding such large budgets demands significant fundraising efforts on the part of most NGOs. Major sources of NGO funding include membership dues, the sale of goods and services, grants from international institutions or national governments, and private donations. Several EU-grants provide funds accessible to NGOs. Even though the term "non-governmental organization" implies independence from governments, most NGOs depend heavily on governments for their funding. A quarter of the US$162 million income in 1998 of the famine-relief organization Oxfam was donated by the British government and the EU. The Christian relief and development organization World Vision collected US$55 million worth of goods in 1998 from the American government. Nobel Prize winner Médecins Sans Frontières (MSF) (known in the USA as Doctors Without Borders) gets 46% of its income from government sources.

Monitoring and Control

In a March 2000 report on United Nations Reform priorities, former U.N. Secretary General Kofi Annan wrote in favour of international humanitarian intervention, arguing that the international community has a "right to protect" citizens of the world against ethnic cleansing, genocide, and crimes against humanity. On the heels of the report, the Canadian government launched the Responsibility to Protect R2PPDF (434 KiB) project, outlining the issue of humanitarian intervention. While the R2P doctrine has wide applications, among the more controversial has been the Canadian government's use of R2P to justify its intervention and support of the coup in Haiti. Years after R2P, the World Federalist Movement, an organization which supports "the creation of democratic global structures accountable to the citizens of the world and call for the division of international authority among separate agencies", has launched Responsibility to Protect-Engaging Civil Society (R2PCS). A collaboration between the WFM and the Canadian government, this project aims to bring NGOs into lockstep with the principles outlined under the original R2P project. The governments of the countries an NGO works or is registered in may require reporting or other monitoring and oversight.

Funders generally require reporting and assessment, such information is not necessarily publicly available. There may also be associations and watchdog organizations that research and publish details on the actions of NGOs working in particular geographic or program areas. In recent years, many large corporations have increased their corporate social responsibility departments in an attempt to preempt NGO campaigns against certain corporate practices. As the logic goes, if corporations work *with* NGOs, NGOs will not work *against* corporations. In December 2007, The United States Department of Defence Assistant Secretary of Defence (Health Affairs) established an International Health Division under Force Health Protection & Readiness.

Part of International Health's mission is to communicate with NGOs in areas of mutual interest. Department of Defence

Directive 3000.05, in 2005, requires DoD to regard stability-enhancing activities as a mission of importance equal to warfighting. In compliance with international law, DoD has necessarily built a capacity to improve essential services in areas of conflict such as Iraq, where the customary lead agencies (State Department and USAID) find it difficult to operate. Unlike the "co-option" strategy described for corporations, the OASD(HA) recognizes the neutrality of health as an essential service. International Health cultivates collaborative relationships with NGOs, albeit at arms-length, recognizing their traditional independence, expertise and honest broker status. While the goals of DoD and NGOs may seem incongruent, the DoD's emphasis on stability and security to reduce and prevent conflict suggests, on careful analysis, important mutual interests.

Legal form of NGOs

The legal form of NGOs is diverse and depends upon homegrown variations in each country's laws and practices. However, four main family groups of NGOs can be found worldwide:

- Unincorporated and voluntary association
- Trusts, charities and foundations
- Companies not just for profit
- Entities formed or registered under special NGO or nonprofit laws.

NGOs are not subjects of international law, as states are. An exception is the International Committee of the Red Cross, which is subject to certain specific matters, mainly relating to the Geneva Convention.

The Council of Europe in Strasbourg drafted the European Convention on the Recognition of the Legal Personality of International Non-Governmental Organizations in 1986, which sets a common legal basis for the existence and work of NGOs in Europe. Article 11 of the European Convention on Human Rights protects the right to freedom of association, which is also a fundamental norm for NGOs.

Citizen Organization

There is a growing movement within the "non"-profit and "non"-government sector to define itself in a more constructive, accurate way. Instead of being defined by "non" words, organizations are suggesting new terminology to describe the sector. The term "civil society organization" (CSO) has been used by a growing number of organizations, such as the Centre for the Study of Global Governance. The term "citizen sector organization" (CSO) has also been advocated to describe the sector — as one of citizens, for citizens. This labels and positions the sector as its own entity, without relying on language used for the government or business sectors. However some have argued that this is not particularly helpful given that most NGOs are in fact funded by governments and business and that some NGOs are clearly hostile to independently organized people's organizations.

STRUCTURES AMONG NGOS

There is a great variety of ways in which NGOs are structured. The classic model is of a membership organization, coordinated in a geographically-defined hierarchy. Individual people work in local groups, which coordinate in provinces and then have a headquarters in the capital city for the country as a whole. Such country-wide organizations are called national NGOs. Frequently, the national NGOs combine in an international NGO, or INGO, which may consist of regional groups of countries and be capped by a global body. Not all the levels of the hierarchy need exist. Many countries are too small to have provincial structures. Smaller specialist

NGOs may simply enrol individual members at the national level, without having any local branches. Occasionally, individuals are enrolled at the international level. On the other hand, in large organizations, the international level often seems relatively remote and attracts little attention, even among the NGO's own members. The group running a local family planning clinic does not necessarily know about the work of the International Planned Parenthood Federation (IPPF) at the UN World Conference on Women in Beijing. Nevertheless, such global organizations with their membership measured in millions do maintain a democratic policy-making process.

While some may hold direct elections for key posts at the national level, the responsibility to the membership at the global level is always indirect, via some international council or assembly of national representatives. It should be noted that one of the ambiguities about the term, NGO, is whether it is referring to a local, provincial, national, regional or global body. Until the early 1990s, the matter was generally straightforward in academic, news media or political discussions. The overwhelming majority of local and provincial NGOs never engaged in transnational activities. Thus NGO, by itself, usually meant a national NGO and regional or global bodies were called international NGOs. National NGOs did engage in transnational development and humanitarian activities, but, with very few exceptions, they were not, in their own right, participants in international diplomacy. When they wanted to exercise political influence at the global level, they did so through the appropriate INGO. In the 1990s, there was a great upsurge in local organizations becoming active at the global level, particularly on environmental issues, because of the Rio Earth Summit in June 1992, and on social issues, because of the Copenhagen Social Summit in March 1995.

Since then, the term INGO has not been used so much and NGO, by itself, has come to cover both national and international NGOs. As an expression of the new politics, various terms then were popularized to refer to local NGOs. Grass-roots organizations, community based organizations (CBOs), and civil society organizations (CSOs), all came into currency. There is still an ambiguity whether these newer terms cover organizations that only operate at the local level or also include local branches of national organizations. Grassroots and community organizations clearly refer solely to the local level, but civil society has connotations of any level within a single country. Indeed, it has become quite common to refer to global civil society. Linguistic usage in the legal atmosphere at the UN used to be somewhat different. When the UN was formed, any involvement of private individuals or groups in its work constituted deviation from the norm of diplomacy being the exclusive preserve of "states". Thus, a national organization, as mentioned in Article 71 of the UN Charter, was any NGO based in a single country. No distinction was made between an organization that covered a large constituency, over the whole country, and an organization based solely in a local community or a small section of the population.

The lack of any distinction did not matter, as participation by either country-wide or more limited national NGOs was so rare in the permanent UN organs. Participation began on a small scale in the 1970s at UN conferences, on an *ad hoc* basis. When the ECOSOC rules were changed in 1996, to admit "national NGOs" to consultative status as a matter of routine, the presumption became that a national organization was a country-wide membership organization or a federation of local groups or an umbrella group, that is a coalition of NGOs operating in different fields. As is common at the UN, practice has not been consistent: a few local NGOs have been admitted as "national NGOs" to consultative status. The Rio conference also produced a term that has only been used in environmental politics at the UN. "Major Groups" refers to a system of categorizing NGOs from all levels, for the purposes of participating in UN policy-making processes. Hereafter, use of NGO alone will imply that any or all levels are included, while local, national or global will be used when the meaning must be restricted to that level. Terms such as CBOs and Major Groups will also be used in the appropriate political context.

A minority of NGOs conform to the model of a global democratic hierarchy, in which any person may become a member. One variant is for the NGO to have subscribers or supporters, providing income, receiving newsletters and responding to calls for action, but not having any democratic control either over expenditure or over policy priorities for the organization. This is common among altruistic NGOs, promoting social welfare and poverty alleviation, and also among environmental NGOs. Another variant is for a specific status or participation in some activity to be a prerequisite for membership.

Thus trade unions are only open to those employed in certain occupations (sometimes very broadly defined). Similarly, professional, scientific and technical bodies are only open to people with the relevant qualification. Such organizations may then be grouped on a functional basis rather than a geographical basis, before they form national and/or international federations. Trade unions do maintain democratic decision-making structures (at least in principle, if not always in practice). However, professional, scientific and technical bodies have professional norms that override democratic norms and members may be expelled for violating the professional norms. A third variant is a religious organization. The major religions do all have complex hierarchies, from the local faith community through to global spiritual authorities. None of them claim to be democratic: authority is based on faith, a holy text, the charisma of individuals or a hierarchical tradition. To some it will be surprising to discuss trade unions, professional bodies and religious organizations as if they are NGOs. Indeed, the leaders of all three will usually deny they are NGOs. Nevertheless, they are treated on the same basis as NGOs throughout the UN system, with the exception of the special place for unions in the International Labour Organisation's tripartite system of governance.

Coalition-Building Among NGOs

Once NGOs do decide to influence public policy, they organize, in broad coalitions, specifically for this purpose. This means there is a large number of NGOs that bear no resemblance to the classic model of a unified hierarchy. Coalitions may take the form of umbrella INGOs, networks or caucuses. In the days when the main form of communication was by mail and even transnational telephone conversations were expensive and time-consuming to arrange, multinational coalitions generally took the form of institutional structures. Many international women's organizations, the International Council of Voluntary Agencies and the World Conservation Union are examples that date from this era.

They are referred to as umbrella organizations, to signify the presence under the single umbrella of a variety of different NGOs that do not share a common identity. In the 1960s, direct transnational telephone dialing was established and air travel became sufficiently cheap for individuals to meet occasionally. Then in the 1970s the news media gradually used satellite communications, so that events in one place were shared around the world as television images. These processes encouraged the formation of looser issue-based networks of NGOs to exchange information, mobilize support and coordinate strategies. At this stage, networks still required some degree of formal organization, with enough resources being raised to pay the salary of a network administrator and associated costs for the paperwork. The International Baby Foods Action Network was the prototype, followed by similar networks on pesticides, rainforests, climate change and other questions.

The advent of e-mail and the web in the 1990s then meant that the costs of running a network dropped substantially and individual people could afford to take part in sophisticated instantaneous global communications. The number of networks increased dramatically and they no longer needed any formal structure. Once a lead organization or even a lead individual establishes technical and political communication skills, a coalition of thousands of NGOs can be formed rapidly and their influence focused on specific targets. The International Campaign to Ban Landmines, the Coalition for an International Criminal Court and Jubilee 2000 are the most spectacular examples. However, the impact of technological change should not be exaggerated. The most effective modern networks still derive their impact from being coalitions of well-organized NGOs. Although communication costs are now minimal, it is still essential to have sufficient resources at the centre, even if they are provided by a single member of the network, for at least one person to devote most or all of his/her time to servicing the network. A variant of the global network is a global caucus.

This arises when a group of NGOs come together as lobbyists at an international diplomatic event, such as a UN agenda-setting conference or a UN forum for negotiating on the formulation or implementation of a treaty. The caucus will be highly focused on achieving specific outcomes from the diplomatic process. The impression is given that such a caucus is an ad hoc grouping that only exists during the two or three weeks of the relevant diplomatic meetings. It may be accurate that the particular combination of NGOs having the particular political purpose will never meet again. However, a successful caucus will be well prepared and will carry forward procedural expertise, substantive knowledge, political status and diplomatic contacts gained in one forum through to the next forum, handling similar questions. Key organizations and key individuals provide continuity.

Women's organizations and environmentalists are among the most successful operating in this way. When we consider something as loose and transient as a caucus, it is perhaps inappropriate to call it an organization. Nevertheless, structured umbrella coalitions, networks and caucuses are all handled in the same way by governments. In the UN system, all transnational actors have to accept the label "NGO", in order to participate. They may be present under the label of the coalition or of its constituents or through both routes. Umbrella INGOs have consultative status and networks usually are listed, but caucuses rarely have any formal recognition. Coalitions that focus on policy outcomes in a particular country or a particular intergovernmental organization will tend to take the form of an umbrella organization. Coalitions that focus on issues tend to take the form of a network or a caucus, with different members being active in different policy forums. In global environmental politics, there is a unique set of caucuses – the system of "Major Groups".

The term was adopted at the Earth Summit, when *Agenda 21* devoted one of its four sections to "Strengthening the Role of Major Groups". The preamble argued that "one of the fundamental prerequisites for the achievement of sustainable development is broad public participation in decision-making" and this must be done as a "real social partnership" with "individuals, groups and organizations". The aim was for the UN to move beyond the traditional reliance on the established NGOs, in two ways. Communication must reach down to individuals at the level of local communities and particular sectors of society of importance for the environment must be mobilized. The section devoted separate chapters to nine Major Groups, under the following headings.

- Strengthening the role of business and industry
- Scientific and technological community
- Strengthening the role of farmers.

The choice of these nine groups was the arbitrary and incoherent outcome of negotiations at UNCED. It was influenced by the personal concerns of Maurice Strong and by the lobbying of NGOs who were accredited to the conference. It is arbitrary to single out women but not men; the young but not the elderly; indigenous people but not other minorities; unions but not professional associations; business and industry but not commerce, finance and services; natural scientists but not social scientists; and farmers but not fishing communities. It is anomalous, but understandable, to emphasize one level of government, local authorities, when they have responsibility for all the Major Groups. Above all it is incoherent to have NGOs as one of the Major Groups, when *all* the other eight (including associations of local authorities) are represented in the UN system via the ECOSOC "arrangements for consultation with non-governmental organizations". This incoherence arises because many in the other Major Groups did not wish to be labelled as NGOs and there had to be a category to encompass environment and development NGOs.

In the Commission on Sustainable Development set up after the Earth Summit, special arrangements were made to allow for participation by all the new groups that had engaged with the UN for the first time at Rio. Any NGO that had been accredited for UNCED was allowed to apply for Roster NGO status at sessions of the CSD and later was given a special fast-track procedure for gaining full status with ECOSOC. Although the CSD is constitutionally a standard subsidiary body of ECOSOC, it has developed its own procedures for relating to NGOs.

Rather than each NGO attempting to exercise its participation rights separately, the NGOs are organized into the nine Major Groups from *Agenda 21*. These categories are used both by the NGOs in their own caucusing and in the formal proceedings. In addition, the CSD has gone beyond the normal consultative arrangements to hold various types of formal, and informal, panels and seminars. Notably, each of the annual sessions starts with the appropriate Major Groups making presentations in special "stakeholder dialogues" on the different substantive agenda items for that year. In pragmatic terms, the illogicality of having NGOs as one of the nine groups of NGOs serves a useful function, in enabling any organization that does not fit elsewhere to be included. This Major Groups system has only operated in the CSD and in other processes that have been derived from UNCED.

THE GEOGRAPHICAL SPREAD OF NGOS

It used to be widely argued that NGOs were predominantly a feature of Western societies. This false proposition was derived from a mixture of ignorance, Western presumptions of their superiority in the Cold War and nationalist rhetoric from authoritarian regimes. All societies in modern times have had large numbers of NGOs at least at the local level. Under the most authoritarian regimes or in the least developed countries there are still self-help cooperative groups, community welfare associations, religious groups, professional and scientific associations, sports and recreational bodies, etc. Even Romania during the dictatorship of President Ceaucescu was host to the International Federation of Beekeepers' Associations. The presence or absence of a democratic political culture is one of the major variables determining the number of NGOs, but the size of a country, its ethnic, religious and cultural diversity, the complexity of its economy and the quality of its communication infrastructure are also of crucial importance.

Thus there are tens of thousands of NGOs in countries such as Bangladesh and India, while there are relatively few in Iceland or Finland. A particular source of controversy is the idea that the major NGOs are "Northern". Many people are still trapped by the mental prejudice that organizations have to be situated in geographical space. It might be a practical necessity for an international NGO to have a headquarters office in a particular building, but the location of the office in a North American or a European city does not convert a global NGO into a Northern NGO. Equally, the historical origins of an organization being formed in a particular country does not mean it is currently a Northern rather than a global organization.

The proper criteria for assessment whether an organization is global are the location of its membership, the staffing of its headquarters, the sources of its funding and the content of its programs. An organization, such as Amnesty International, with 56 National Sections, groups in some 40 other countries, an International Secretariat from over 50 countries and an African Secretary-General is a global NGO, even if it started in Britain and has its headquarters in London. Due to the spread of democracy and the improvements in communications, many international NGOs that started in individual countries became global at the end of the twentieth century.

TYPES OF NGO ACTIVITIES

Much as observers wish to gain greater understanding by defining different categories of NGOs, it is not possible to do so. We may distinguish different activities, but specific NGOs will often change the balance of the activities they pursue. The most common distinction is between operational and campaigning NGOs. This may be interpreted as the choice between small-scale change achieved directly through projects and large-scale change promoted indirectly through influence on the political system. Operational NGOs have to mobilize resources, in the form of financial donations, materials or volunteer labour, in order to sustain their projects and programs.

This process may require quite complex organization. Charity shops, staffed by volunteers, in premises provided at nominal rents and selling donated goods, end up providing finance to the national headquarters. Students in their vacations or during a break in their education provide labour for projects. Finance obtained from grants or contracts, from governments, foundations or companies, require time and expertise spent on planning, preparing applications, budgeting, accounting and reporting. Major fund-raising events require skills in advertising, media relations and motivating supporters. Thus, operational NGOs need to possess an efficient headquarters bureaucracy, in addition to the operational staff in the field. Campaigning NGOs will carry out much the same functions, but with a different balance between them. Fund-raising is still necessary, but on a smaller scale and it can serve the symbolic function of strengthening the donors' identification with the cause. Persuading people to donate their time is necessary, but, in addition to a small number of people giving a great deal of time, it is also necessary to be able to mobilize large numbers for brief periods. External donors may not impose onerous administrative burdens, but supporters still have to be supplied with information on an efficient regular basis.

Major events will aim to attract favourable publicity rather than raise funds. Therefore, despite their differences, both operational and campaigning NGOs need to engage in fund-raising, mobilization of work by supporters, organizing special events, cultivating the media and administering a headquarters. Only the defining activities – implementing projects or holding demonstrations – serve to differentiate them. In reality, the distinctions are not as sharp as the labels suggest. Operational NGOs often move into campaigning when projects regularly face similar problems and the impact of the projects seems to be insufficient. All the large development and environment operational NGOs now run some regular campaigns, at least by supporting campaigning networks. Similarly, campaigning NGOs often feel they cannot ignore the immediate practical problems of people in their policy domain. Human rights NGOs and women's NGOs end up having programs to assist the victims of discrimination and injustice. Various other types of NGOs can be regarded as promoting change by variants on these two primary functions.

Research institutes have special forms of operational programs, in which the goal is to increase knowledge and understanding. They range across a spectrum from those promoting an academic, non-political image to those collating and disseminating information for campaigning purposes. Professional bodies, trade unions, recreational groups and associations of companies provide program activities required by and for their members, but they may also campaign to enhance the economic interests and the status of their organizations. These categories and several others have some practical value for everyday discourse, but they do not provide the basis for an analytical classification of NGOs. The most effective way to distinguish between NGOs is to obtain precise data on a range of different variables.

The number of full-time employees, the number of members and the funding of the annual budget give measures of the size of any NGO. Opinion poll data on recognition of and support for an NGO or its goals, along with the frequency of positive mentions in the news media, give measures of its political strength. There are also more subjective variables, such as the professional skill, knowledge and experience of the personnel, that matter for both operational and campaigning purposes.

UNDERSTANDING STRATEGIC ROLE OF NGOS

UR world encounters one of the biggest economic crisis in its history. Some of the companies face bankruptcies as a result of this challenging economic crisis. On the other hand, some companies do not show too much negative signs in terms of their performances (e.g., sales, market value, profits, assets, and market value) as a result of global economic crisis. This fact is very obvious when the firms in the lists of Fortune Magazine's World's Most Admired Companies and Forbes Magazine's Global 2000 Most Reputable Companies are examined carefully. It is obvious in these two famous lists that most of these firms that are shown as the world's most admired companies by Fortune also appear in the list of Forbes Magazine's Most Reputable Companies. One of the most important strategies of these companies is their relationships with the important NGOs that monitor them closely.

There are five major variables (network relationships, cooperative behaviours, corporate reputation, immunization to crisis and sustainable growth) that determine the relationships between firms and NGOs. First, these five variables will be explained in details. Second, some of the cases about cooperative relationships between NGOs and firms will be presented. Finally, implications of these relationships will be interpreted based on these five variables. Besides, the important role of NGOs that initiates information flows among stakeholder group and organized actions about firms (i.e., NGOs play the role of catalyst among stakeholders and firms) will also be presented in this paper.

NETWORK RELATIONSHIPS

The multilateral relationships among firms and their stakeholders refer to the process of network relationships. Today, any bad or good news that is done to the members of a stakeholder group quickly spreads to other stakeholder groups. If stakeholders of a firm do not like the action of a firm, it can find itself in public relations nightmare that can threaten its existence. The increase in communication among stakeholders via internet makes companies more visible. These multiple and interdependent interactions among the network of stakeholders constitutes the firm. This phenomenon is called as the network relationships.

There are many multilateral interactions among stakeholders in and around firms. Thus, management scholars and managers recognize that there are complex interactions and network effects between the firm and its stakeholders. Therefore, finding ways or strategies to manage the communication across stakeholder groups is the most important issue in today's business world. NGOs may have a central role in terms of initiating network relationships among stakeholder groups. When pressure groups (NGOs) protest the unethical behaviours of a firm, they also initiate the flow of information about the relevant firm's behaviours (i.e. they initiate network relationships among them). In other words, NGOs are catalyst to enhance the communication and to initiate network relationships among firms' stakeholders. The process of network relationships has emerged as a result of development in communication technologies and NGOs, which eased the information flows among the stakeholder groups. In sum, NGOs are bridge between firms and stakeholders.

IMPORTANCE OF NGOS IN BUSINESS LIFE

NGOs will play the role of catalyst in the 21st century. Since the cost of communication has dropped dramatically due to vast use of Internet, the increase in communication among stakeholders via Internet makes firms more visible. Therefore, any bad or good news about firms in any place of the world can be learned easily by the stakeholders of firms via communication technologies. Stakeholders can react to these events instantly but these reactions do not affect firms if they are dispersed. There are many events which show us that only organized reactions of stakeholders can produce effective results in terms of influencing firms. NGOs have a central role in creating these organized reactions that are used for making firms to work for the benefits of their stakeholders. Since firms cannot exist without the support of their stakeholders, firms are expected to work for the benefits of their stakeholders by the help of NGOs. According to the Edelman's Trust Barometer in 2008 and 2009, NGOs are the most trusted institutions in the world. Based on these facts, it would not be wrong to argue that NGOs have an important role in the business life.

COOPERATIVE BEHAVIOURS

When a firm moves with its stakeholders or when a firm forms collaborative relationships with its stakeholders or when employees contribute voluntarily to a firm or when there is a collective action between the managers and employees or when there is an unity of action in the organization or when a firm honours its contracts, cooperates in joint efforts and delivers on time, the process of cooperative behaviours emerges in and around firm. The most effective strategy to form cooperative behaviours with the stakeholders is to cooperate with the well known NGOs such as World Wildlife Fund (WWF) or GreenPeace or World Resources Institute so that they will always spread good news about your company rather than bad ones. The most important mission of the NGOs is to serve to the needs of the civil society. Thus, well-known independent NGOs are expected to pursue the interests of society and monitor companies to achieve this mission. In other words, NGOs are bridge between firms and their stakeholders. In sum, if firms want to develop a sound strategy in terms of responding to the needs of their stakeholders, they are expected to form cooperative behaviours (e.g. being an environment friendly company or producing high qualified products) with the wellknown independent NGOs.

Good Corporate Reputation

The importance of generating a good corporate reputation is emphasized by some scholars. When a firm wins broad public acceptance in a complex business environment, good corporate reputation emerges as a business result. A good reputation, which emerges when stakeholders have a positive opinion about the firm, is very important for the firms because it can act as a buffer when things go wrong. A good corporate reputation may also aid to the customer loyalty and foster the feeling of trust between a firm and its stakeholders. When organizations build good reputation, they also reduce the costs of social controls. In sum, good corporate reputation is an important intangible asset in especially bad times.

Immunization to Crisis

When a firm preserves its license to operate in changing circumstances or when a firm is resilient to short-term shocks or crises, we talk about a firm's immunization to crisis as a business outcome. For example, a good reputation is very important for firms because it can act as a buffer when things go wrong. When the turbulent environment around the firms during recent global economic crisis is considered, a good reputation makes more sense for these firms because they have the chance to immunize themselves to economic crises or shocks by having a good corporate reputation.

Sustainable Growth

Sustainable growth of firms is the concern of many scholars. Constituting an ongoing growth of a firm is the definition for the sustainable growth as a business result. A stakeholder inclusive firm is expected to achieve sustainable growth. Stakeholder perspective posits that forming good relationships with critical stakeholders leads to sustainable growth over time. Firms are expected to achieve sustainable growth by forming systematic communication or establishing active communication with their stakeholders. Of course, the principle of mutual-interests is the underlying reason for sustainable growth as a business outcome. If a firm can align the interests of its stakeholders, sustainable growth of the firm can be constituted.

The importance of good corporate reputation can be seen during economic shocks or crisis. Firms that understand the importance of network relationships and form cooperative behaviours with the NGOs will be the ones that will achieve a good corporate reputation in the long term. Therefore, firms that achieve a good corporate reputation are expected to produce better financial performance than the ones that ignore the importance of network relationships and cooperative behaviours with the well-known NGOs and produce a bad corporate reputation as a business outcome. In sum, firms that can achieve sustainable growth in the long term by emphasizing right relationships with the NGOs will more likely be the ones that will survive and prosper even during the economic shocks and crisis.

Cooperation Between Firms and NGOs

United States Climate Action Programme (USCAP) is an expanding alliance of major businesses and leading climate and environmental groups (i.e., NGOs) in United States that have come together to call on the federal government to enact legislation requiring significant reductions of greenhouse gas emissions. There are well-known companies such as General Electric, Protecter & Gamble, DuPont and CaterPillar among the founder companies of USCAP. There are four climate and environmental groups (Environmental Defence, Natural Resources Defence Council, Pew Center Global Climate Change, and World Resources Institute) among the founder NGOs. This cooperation between the NGOs and firms to reduce the gas emmision %80 until 2050 creates a good corporate reputation on the eyes of stakeholders because climate change is one of the most important issues in the 21st century. Climate Savers Programme is another collaboration between World Wildlife Fund (WWF) and the world's leading companies such as IBM, HP, Johnson & Johnson, Nokia and Sony. The purpose of these collaboration is to deal with climate change issue by reducing the gas emmissions. All of these companies are aware of the fact that commitment on reducing gas emmisions will increase their costs but they are also aware of the fact that the increase in their revenues due to compliance with the interests of society will be sustainable. These companies are also aware of the fact that compliance with the interests of the society will create a good reputation on the eyes of their stakeholders (i.e., these companies are aware of the fact that their existence depends on their compliance with the interests of their stakeholders such as protecting the environment). When we look at the financial figures of some of these companies, these kinds of firms also still perform well during the global economic crisis. Thus, following a strategy, which is based on the cooperative behaviours with the NGOs, has created a good corporate reputation for these firms that act as a buffer during the global economic crisis (i.e. immunization to crisis).

The recent global economic crisis has led to bankruptcies of many well known companies. On the other hand, there are firms that still perform well during this crisis. Firms that cooperate with the well-known NGOs also serve well to the needs of their stakeholders, which is very important for their survival. Firms are aware of the fact that they are surrounded by the network of stakeholder groups, which are organized by the NGOs. Besides, firms are well aware of the fact that NGOs play the role of a catalyst among stakeholders for the related information flows and organized actions about firms. Thus, some of the firms choose to cooperate with the NGOs so that stakeholders of these firms are satisfied with these firms' activities and they continue their transactions with these kinds of firms even in bad times. In other words, these firms are well aware of the fact that their cooperation with the NGOs is expected to create sustainable growth and a good corporate reputation for them in the long term. Therefore, it will be these kinds of corporations that will survive and prosper during the global economic crisis. When the performance (e.g., Sales, market value, profits, assets, and market value) results of these firms are examined, it can be seen that the most admired and reputable firms in the world are the ones that still perform well during recent the global economic crisis.

2

NGO Accountability: Introducing Political Responsibility

Advocacy is most clearly seen in the context of global campaigns, generally carried out by NGO networks or NGOs working in a loose alliance. These campaigns challenge projects, policies and political forces which threaten to further marginalize local communities or ruin pristine ecosystems. There are political responsibilities which are inherent to taking part in these advocacy campaigns.

Political responsibility is generally understood as something which derives from the act of representation. Yet many NGOs deny the concept of representation, pointing out that local communities are able to adequately represent themselves. NGOs generally feel more comfortable describing themselves as information brokers or issue-oriented advocacy groups, but not as representative entities. We question this position. While it is true that local communities are often able to adequately present their own interests, local leaders or spokespersons are often tied to the local geographical space within which they live. They do not have daily access to other politically important geographical spaces like national capitals, or internationally important political spaces such as Washington D.C., New York, Brussels, Hong Kong or Nairobi. Nor have they invested the time required to understand the mechanics of investment banks, the United Nations, etc. We call these differing political spaces where decision making takes place 'political arenas'. In advocacy, local communities or NGOs often call upon NGOs elsewhere to articulate their concerns in political arenas which they do not know or cannot reach themselves. With the globalization of decision making on the increase, we can only expect that the need to articulate concerns in more than one political arena will continue to grow. A democracy deficit is on the rise precisely because of the dispersed nature of decision making across national borders. NGOs, by organizing advocacy campaigns in different political arenas at the same time, try to address this democracy deficit, either implicitly or explicitly. While cooperation in an advocacy campaign does not easily compare itself to academic concepts of representation, it cannot be denied that NGOs are in fact representing interests when they operate with a specific expertise geared towards a specific political arena and using that knowledge to carry a campaign issue to a new level of decision making. The sheer fact of participation in a global campaign or in an NGO network, embodies a political responsibility. One can think about it as representation or participation, regardless, it is an act with inherent political responsibilities.

A key problem in political responsibility is that international NGO networks constitute both direct participation and an unusual form of political representation. Beginning with the political representation issue, the concept of political representation as we know it embodies a one-to-one relationship between the representative, be it a person or an organization, and a constituency defined by a concrete geographical space and an equally concrete body with political power. The mandate of a member of parliament is limited by national boundaries. The mandate of the cadre of a labour union is equally limited by the boundaries within which her members are living, who gave her the mandate to negotiate with the private corporation that employs the members.

This one-to-one relationship between the representative and the represented takes on a multiple anatomy within international NGO networks. NGO networks bridge geographical spaces as well as institutional gaps and operate in different political arenas at the same time. The checks and balances established by NGO networks must flow through multiple political arenas and cover institutional gaps. Only then are they meaningful for people in a particular local situation, and embody the possibility to establish a form of consent with regard to a particular decision. These are essential elements in the application of democratic principles. What is created in NGO networks is a form of representation which, in its optimal version, is shifting from local to national to international levels and vice versa, in accordance with the objectives of the campaign. In an era of global political realities but no global system of checks and balances, democracy has to stand up and walk.

Political responsibility in NGO advocacy manifests itself in the following seven areas:

1. dividing political arenas;
2. agenda setting and strategy building;

3. raising and allocating financial resources;
4. information flow;
5. information frequency and format;
6. information translation into useful forms;
7. the formalization of relationships.

In each area there are parameters by which political responsibility can be assessed. The sum of all actions combined can help NGOs to measure the extent to which they have successfully managed political risks and embraced their political responsibilities. While in case materials below, we have predominantly used examples of environmental campaigns to further illustrate our arguments, these areas of political responsibility arise in any development action which utilizes more than one political arena. In any action whereby an international and a locally based organization are engaged, be it a food delivery service in an emergency situation or an agriculture extension service, these responsibilities arise, regardless of the nature of the partnership between beneficiaries and NGOs.

Dividing Political Arenas

From the outset of becoming involved in advocacy it is important to explicitly recognize that there are various political arenas in which each NGO operates. It is typical for an international campaign to grow from the need to engage more than one political arena. And no one group generally has the understanding of each arena that needs to be engaged. For example, it cannot be expected that a grassroots social movement organization in the hinterland of India will know all of the politically important people in Washington D.C., will understand the protocol associated with contacting relevant decision makers, or will have the resources to bring pressure to bear in that political arena. The opposite is true as well. Organizations based in Washington, New York or Geneva may be intimately familiar with the way in which those arenas work and how decisions are made, but will not be able to understand the pace, the mechanisms or the reality of a local situation in Africa. Many readers may interpret our division of arenas to be a North-South division. That is not the case. Expertise in a political arena is based upon a long term presence in that arena. Thus, FAVDO, which is an African based organization, maintains a presence in Washington D.C. and thus has expertise in the Washington arena that we would argue should be respected by partner organizations when practising advocacy. Recognizing who has expertise and knowledge in which political arena and respecting the boundaries established by that expertise is the first necessary act of accountability in a joint NGO advocacy effort. By recognizing the boundaries within which each NGO prevails, campaign activists go a long way towards recognizing the political responsibility in advocacy.

Agenda setting and strategy building

The second major issue which NGOs need to engage is the question of agenda setting and strategy building. What are the substantive priorities, for whose benefit, using which time frame and with what level of antagonism are authorities or power holders approached in which political arena? These are some of the questions which need to be answered, pointing at the fact that agenda setting and strategy building is closely related to the management of risks. Tactics and strategies decided upon can have major consequences for all actors involved. Agendas in advocacy will vary depending upon the objectives of each NGO. It is therefore essential to find a format to lay out explicitly what one's objectives are and to then develop a strategy with transparent goals. Among the issues which need to be recognized is who bears the risks associated with campaign positions or even with project failure. (This is particularly relevant in the case of service delivery.) Not surprisingly, often specific attention is needed for the partner organization in the campaign who has fewer resources or has to deal with a repressive regime.

Allocation of available financial resources

The need for financial resources varies from arena to arena. The availability of financial resources is a major factor contributing to the risk of lopsided relationships among NGOs around the globe, as the bulk of financial resources is in the hands of a relatively small group of NGOs in the North. Prioritizing expenses is an issue which can cause tension among organizations. Determining who has money and can pay for activities, who has access to other sources of financing and who cannot contribute financially to the activities agreed upon is one step towards recognizing the relationships of power which money generates among NGOs. A rough review of a number of NGO networks and relationships we have been involved in has taught us that it helps for more powerful, i.e. financially resourceful, organizations to clearly separate the responsibility for raising and appropriating money from advocacy. Financial accountability and political responsibility are different and should not be confused in management.

Information flow: In advocacy, information is the most powerful tool. In social service delivery, information is critical to decision making; for example, when determining where the most vulnerable or needy group is located, what kind of services are required and when prioritizing these needs over the needs of other groups elsewhere. The direction in which the information flows between and among different NGOs, whether all participants in an advocacy campaign have equal access to the same information, the density of the flow of information and the quality of available information will all have an impact on the level of accountability. The ability to actually analyse, process or generate information is equally important.

Information frequency and format

The frequency with which NGOs relay information to one another is not only important in the context of the management of political responsibilities, but also in the effectiveness of the same campaign. Significant events can erupt at any given moment and can either positively or adversely affect any member of a campaign. Getting information out can help other partners in the campaign to be prepared and/or protected. Equally important is to determine an appropriate mix of communication formats. The necessary trust to seriously discuss agenda setting, strategies and risk-management cannot be developed by Email alone (if it is available). Again, certain participants in the advocacy effort at hand may prefer to speak rather than write, which requires using the phone, while a certain frequency of meetings in person will also be inevitable, preferably including meetings in the political arena(s) where the most urgent problems occur.

Articulating information into useful forms

Information by itself is not enough to pursue effective advocacy. Often the available information needs interpretation in accordance with the political arena in which it is being articulated. For example, World Bank documents and Indian newspaper articles are equally difficult to understand unless they are translated for the reader who is familiar with neither the institution nor the political arena. Pointing out the critical statements or aspects of the documentation to fellow activists in other political arenas, translating the important pieces of information (either from the local language into English or vice-versa), are critical aspects of accountability. In many situations, oral communication is the only method of communication which is effective at a local level. A key indicator of accountability in NGO advocacy is the lengths to which NGOs will go to break through communication and language barriers.

The formalization of relationships

In advocacy campaigns relationships between and among NGOs are often fluid. Advocacy campaigns on the international level take time to determine who is going to be involved in the issue. As campaigns develop, relationships tend to become more formalized. They can even get to the point where they have statutes such as in the case of World Rainforest Movement (WRM) or the International NGO Forum on Indonesian Development (INFID). Action committees, a memorandum of understanding, the production of joint newsletters etc. represent varying levels of formalization of mutual relationships in NGO advocacy. Formalization can help to establish transparency, which is another key issue in advocacy. Transparency is a very valuable tool in that it often highlights the lack of transparency in counter forces.

Recognizing and clearly establishing the parameters of mutual relationships among NGOs involved in an advocacy effort can help in defining political responsibilities, certainly if the relationships in question are expected to be productive over a longer period. The more parameters that are defined, the more explicit the level of accountability and the better that risks can be managed.

TYPOLOGIES OF NGO RELATIONSHIPS IN ADVOCACY

Coming face-to-face with the political responsibility inherent in NGO advocacy is not easy. The areas demarcated in the previous section are intended to help NGOs recognize the parameters of their relationships as they may develop in an advocacy setting, and in particular across national boundaries. Below, we suggest four typologies of NGO relationships to contextualize the political responsibilities inherent to NGO advocacy. These four typologies are highlighted by campaign case studies meant to illuminate the above areas in practice. They are not meant to be the definitive historical description of what happened in each of these cases. Nor do we explore the success or failures of these campaigns vis-a-vis their ultimate goals or objectives. The sole purpose of suggesting these typologies is to further elaborate our argument and to propose an additional tool for NGOs to come to terms with the political responsibility in NGO advocacy. The typologies in this section are based on a condensed version of the seven areas of political responsibility which we have identified in the previous section. In our typologies we match the commensurability of different objectives of an advocacy campaign in different political arenas with a qualification of what happens with information and how strategies, risks and funds are managed. The level of accountability in each typology is an outcome of these indicators. An overview of the four typologies is given at the end of this section.

The Hybrid Campaign

We call our first typology of relationships among NGOs engaged in advocacy a "hybrid campaign". In a hybrid campaign, the level of accountability towards the most politically vulnerable actors is at its peak. For the most part, advocacy agendas and strategies are set in close consultation with the groups who are supposed to benefit from the campaign and risks are assumed only in regard to the burden that can be born by the most vulnerable. There are four dynamics which frame the typology:

- *a representation of interlocking objectives by different NGOs in multiple political arenas is intertwined;*
- *a very fluid and continuous flow of information among all NGOs involved;*
- *a continuous review of strategies and joint management of political responsibilities by all NGOs involved. Risk management is purely based on local realities in the political arena where participants in the campaign are most vulnerable;*
- *a high level of accountability.*

To highlight the parameters of political responsibility in a hybrid campaign we take the relatively well-known case of Narmada as an example. The Narmada campaign had a high level of accountability among campaigners in our view because the above four factors were achieved. The objectives of each set of actors in their own political arena were clearly defined, understood and eventually intertwined. There was a fluid and continuous flow of information among all actors involved. There was a continuous review of strategies and joint management of political responsibilities by all actors involved. Risk management was based upon the strength of the most politically exposed.

By way of providing the reader with a very brief history, the Sardar Sarovar dam in India came under controversy from its inception in the early 1980's. The project became controversial because in its original formulation it would have resulted in the flooding of the traditional lands of over 250,000 tribal people living on the banks of the Narmada river in Gujarat, Madhya Pradesh and Maharashtra. In total, over one million people were expected to be affected. The NGO campaign to stop the dam became an international campaign when the World Bank agreed to finance the construction of the Sardar Sarovar dam.

On the local level, the objectives of the tribal people were first limited to obtaining proper resettlement compensation. On the international level, the destruction of pristine wildlife areas motivated the first campaigners in countries other than India to raise their voice. The concern for the environment, however, was quickly blurred by a concern for the rights of the tribals. Once it became clear that the authorities involved would not be able to properly compensate 'oustees', the campaign on the local level became an anti-dam campaign. Gradually the anti-dam message filtered through to the international campaign.

The targets of the various actors in the campaign differed from the outset. The tribals targeted the national state of India and the three states involved in the project. The tribals employed national NGOs in India, based in New Delhi, to help influence both national level ministries and as the campaign developed, the national court system. International actors targeted national bilateral aid programs and the World Bank. Each actor in the campaign concentrated on their own political arena, developing dialogues and tactics specific to those arenas. However, there were many instances where shows of mutual solidarity worked best and thus there were many instances when actors visited other political arenas than their own. The purposes of these visits were either to tell their own stories, as in the case of the tribals coming to Washington, or to better understand the realities and threats at the local level and to provide protection to those who were politically exposed, as was the case when international actors went to the Narmada Valley. While the varying political arenas were shared, the strength of each set of actors in specific arenas was recognized and respected. Overlap was by invitation only. In the Narmada campaign, advocacy agendas of different NGOs were varied: to seek proper compensation for the tribals; to get the Bank out of the project; to stop other governments from supporting the project; to expose the Bank's failure to be able to abide by its own policies; to expose the State governments' failures to abide by their policies and to ultimately stop the construction of the dam. Not all of these agendas were shared on the tactical level. But, all agendas were repeatedly discussed among the various actors involved and agreed upon. Different tactics were developed in the different political arenas and regularly shared.

A Narmada Action Committee (NAC) was established on the international level to keep communication flowing and to highlight new events and decisions taken in the Narmada Valley. The NAC fulfilled not only information needs but also established a level of responsibility to the tribals from many centres around the world. The tribals knew they could call collect to Amsterdam or Washington and their requests would be heard all over the world within a matter of hours. The NAC also helped people share in decision making. Generally, once a year, actors would meet to compare notes; to reaffirm their interest in the case; and to hear from someone who may have just arrived from the Valley. In this way, the global relationships among international campaigners active in the Narmada case was somewhat formalized. The lines of communication were relatively clear; the frequency of communication was substantial; the responsibility of each actor to the local arena and to one another was clear. Similar mechanisms were employed between the national level in India and the local arenas. Information generated on the international level was translated into tribal languages while the Narmada Bachao Andolan produced updates of local facts and events for the international NGO community on a regular basis. These were often handwritten bulletins faxed to Washington and then distributed globally.

When particular activists might be tempted to go too far with a strategy, the threat of being cut off from the primary sources of information and the threat of being ostracized by the movement in the Narmada Valley was used. Futhermore, decisions made in the most politically vulnerable arena were respected by all players. When the actors in the local arena chose not to participate in an academic study about the movement, all international actors abided by that decision and did not cooperate. The Narmada case was special in that money did not flow between various arenas. Money from the international arena was considered to be more harmful than helpful for the tribals. However, resources were shared. For example, faxes were paid for by the international organizations, telephone calls were made with charges being paid by wealthier NGOs, etc. Money hardly ever crossed from one political arena into another. This dissipated any unhealthy power relationships that might have developed in the campaign.

The Concurrent Campaign

Our second typology of relationships among NGOs which are engaged in advocacy is the "concurrent campaign". The concurrent campaign has coinciding representation of different but compatible objectives. It does not achieve a high level of accountability given that the objectives in various political arenas are different. Thus, information loops are not as tight as they would be in a hybrid campaign where everything is intertwined and direction is taken from the most politically exposed. The dynamics of a concurrent campaign can be qualified as follows:

- *a coinciding representation of different but compatible objectives by NGOs operating in their own political arena;*
- *a regular but multi-phased flow of information among NGOs involved;*
- *a frequent review of strategies and coexisting management of political responsibilities by varying combinations of NGOs involved at different levels;*
- *a medium level of accountability.*

We present the Arun Dam campaign as an example of a concurrent campaign. The Arun III was a Japanese-conceived run-of-the-river dam project scheduled to be built in a remote area of Nepal, the Arun valley. The valley, while relatively sparsely populated, contained an eco-system rich in biodiversity. The dam was hydroelectric and meant to supply energy to two major city centres in Nepal and the rest to India. The total cost of the project (over a decade) was estimated at US$ 764 million, about the size of Nepal's annual national budget.

In the Arun case the objectives of NGOs in different political arenas varied. On the national level in Nepal, the Arun case was an anti-dam campaign from the outset. The issues advocated upon were purely environmental and economic. At the international level, the case was also anti-dam, predominantly because of its environmental impact. The case in part, however, became an international one because it arose at a time which coincided with the creation of the World Bank's Inspection Panel. The planned participation of the World Bank in the financing of the Arum Dam thus provided an opportunity to test the new inspection mechanism. These objectives were well understood by all actors and were not in conflict with one another. In fact, it was the national level actors who chose to use the Inspection Mechanism as an additional advocacy tool. Nevertheless, the possibility of using the mechanism generated interest in the case at international levels to a greater extent than before. Overlap in the objectives occurred in the writing of the inspection claim, where the economic arguments favoured by the local people were predominant, next to alleging violations of environmental assessment, resettlement and other World Bank policies. After the Inspection Panel had completed a review of the project, newly appointed World Bank President Wolfensohn announced in August 1995 that the Bank would no longer support Arun III, thereby effectively killing the project.

The flow of information in the Arun case was specific as opposed to all-encompassing in the Narmada case. Information flowed between various actors but not across, so that the Nepalese were responsible for communicating with each and every contact made at the international level (as opposed to the contacts flowing between and among international players). Relationships between campaigners internationally were less formal than in the Narmada case. On the national level in Nepal, however, relationships were formalized by establishing two NGO coalitions, the Alliance for Energy and the Arun Concerned Group. The connections to the local arena were weak in the Arun case so theories about the needs and desires of the local people were not very well tested. This was the greatest weakness of the campaign. There was a low level of maintaining political responsibility with respect to the local region. As a result, when the World Bank's decision to withdraw from the project was announced, the Nepalese NGOs initially were afraid to openly show their satisfaction as they feared a backlash from some local interest groups who had anticipated to benefit from the project. At the same time, international NGOs were releasing a statement which presumed that Nepalese people were dancing in the street.

The Disassociated Campaign

The third typology to qualify the relationships among NGOs engaged in advocacy we call the "disassociated campaign". This type of campaign takes us one step further away from truly interwoven relationships among NGOs, to a situation where-based upon the same issue-advocacy objectives represented by various NGOs in different political arenas begin to clash.

The dynamics of the typology are:

- *parallel representation of conflicting objectives by different NGOs in their own political arena;*
- *a regular but lopsided flow of information among the NGOs involved, usually more information flows from the South to the North rather than vice versa;*

- *occasional and unaffiliated review of strategies and management of political responsibilities among different NGOs involved, predominantly exclusive to their own political arena;*
- *a low level of accountability.*

The example we use to illustrate the typology of a disassociated campaign is the intended investment of the US Scott Paper company in a pulp and paper plantation in Irian Jaya, East Indonesia. Like the previous cases, environmental concerns and issues of peoples' participation were at the forefront of the NGO agenda(s). However, next to national and provincial authorities, the main target of the campaign was a private company rather than the World Bank. In October 1988, the US-based Scott Paper company announced a US$ 653.8 million investment in a tree farm and pulp mill project in the South Eastern part of Irian Jaya. The project was to be realized by means of a joint venture between Scott Paper and PT Astra, a large Indonesian conglomerate, well connected to the Indonesian regime. The aim of the project was to gradually establish a eucalyptus plantation of up to 200,000 hectares to provide logs for a pulp and wood factory in nearby Merauke.

Soon after the public announcement of the project, local and national NGOs began to put forward criticisms and demands. The Indonesian Network for Forest Conservation (Skephi) led a coalition with 9 other Indonesian Jakarta-based NGOs, who began to raise concerns. Skephi questioned how a forest concession could have been granted to PT Astra Scott Cellulosa without the implementation of an Environmental Impact Assessment in conformity with Indonesian Environmental Law. Other issues raised by Indonesian NGOs were: how Scott and Astra planned to involve local communities in the project, especially with respect to the use of tribal land; the impact on customary land ownership; the selection of pristine tropical rain forest (which would lead to the destruction of genetic resources, while the resulting deforestation could lead to the drying up of natural rivers); the composition of the necessary labour force and how it would be recruited; and whether upstream and downstream wastes would be handled appropriately. NGOs in the US took over these demands.

In response to initial NGO criticism, Scott promised an environmental as well as a social impact assessment, and explained that there would be an extended test-period for the project to review its environmental and social soundness. The company stated that the intention was to carefully approach the project. The relationship with the local communities was described as a "win-win" situation with promises being made as to the creation of 6000 jobs, training for local people, as well as the provision of schools and medical facilities.

Subsequently, communication between Scott and NGOs developed on various levels, primarily in Irian Jaya and in the US. A group of five local NGOs got together and established fairly regular communication with representatives of PT Astra Scott Cellulosa. The local NGOs got hold of a copy of the project plans, which they translated into Indonesian and circulated among local communities. NGOs were assigned to help explain and discuss the documents and the project in general with the local communities, in a series of meetings which were organized by the NGOs. The local district authorities also got involved in these meetings.

In the course of 1989, an agenda for local NGOs emerged, in which they basically accepted the establishment of the plantation, trying to gain training and employment opportunities, fair compensation for tribal land and proper control over environmental, social and cultural impacts. The discussions with Scott went as far as the establishment of an agreement to keep away prostitution and bars from the project area. With respect to the important question of land ownership, Scott started making a map of the project area using village maps, as opposed to using official maps which did not properly reflect traditional land ownership. The local communities also expressed a preference to lease — rather than sell — their land, which Scott was willing to discuss. Part of the financing of the local level negotiations and capacity building efforts was provided for by USAID and the Asia Foundation.

Meanwhile, at the international level, an NGO campaign with a different character had emerged. The project in Irian Jaya was framed by linking Scott Paper to their responsibility for environmental damage in the US and Canada. Scott Paper in the U.S. and its subsidiaries in Europe were vigorously targeted by a number of NGOs, like the Rainforest Action Network (RAN) and Survival International. NGOs threatened a consumers' boycott of Scott Products if Scott would not leave pristine rain forest and the areas of tribal people untouched. These NGOs cooperated in particular with the Skephi led coalition in Indonesia. Some Jakarta based NGOs and some international groups, such as the Indonesian Environmental Forum (WALHI) and the Environmental Defence Fund (EDF), tried to follow a road in between. They communicated in a less aggressive way with the Scott Paper company and stated to be willing to accept the project, as long as a number of demands were met. While NGOs at the international level communicated intensively with each other, there was not much communication between the local and international levels of the NGO campaign. International groups suspected that local people were in fact not well informed and were already worn-out by years of Indonesian oppression and intimidation in this remote region of Irian Jaya. This perception was strengthened by the decision of the Indonesian government to virtually close off the area to outsiders.

The situation climaxed in the second half of 1989. The Scott Paper project was one of the cases highlighted by RAN in a full-page advertisement in the New York Times, pointing at the destruction of tropical rain forest. On October 13, Scott announced its withdrawal from the project, apparently quite to the surprise of PT Astra and the Indonesian authorities, who had already boosted the overall data of foreign investment in Indonesia in 1989 by including the project in Irian Jaya. The reason for the withdrawal given by Scott was that "extensive studies now indicate the Company can meet its anticipated needs for pulp from other sources". However, in interviews, Scott agreed that NGO pressure played an important role in the considerations of the company to withdraw. The differences between NGOs operating at different levels in appreciating the outcome of the campaign, were best summed up in a letter from a local NGO to Survival International after Scott's withdrawal. The local NGO agreed that it would be best if the project would be stopped altogether. But PT Astra and the Indonesian authorities had already announced that negotiations with various new potential foreign counterparts for the project were on the way. What would the international NGOs do, was the question from East Irian Jaya, when a new company from Japan, Taiwan or Korea would enter the local arena, most likely much less willing to negotiate with the local communities or NGOs as compared to Scott Paper?

The Competitive Campaign

Our fourth typology provides the worst case scenario, the "competitive campaign". In this situation, advocacy on one level may actually have an adverse or counterproductive impact at another level. There is a serious lack of information exchange and coordination among the NGOs involved, resulting in an absence of accountability and a failure to embrace political responsibilities. The dynamics of the competitive campaign are:

- *parallel representation of opposing objectives by different NGOs in different political arenas*;
- *no direct flow of information among different NGOs at different levels*;
- *no joint review of strategies or management of political responsibilities which may result in human rights violations or other negative impacts on the interests of local communities;*
- *no accountability.*

As an example of a competitive campaign we take the case of the Huaorani fighting against American oil interests in Ecuador. Since 1967 American oil companies have exploited oil resources in Ecuador with impunity. Leaking pipelines, oil-fires, violence and intimidation have all been part of the operational realities in search for the black gold. Rainforests and thriving tribal communities have been destroyed by the practices of Texaco and Petroecuador. In the battle to keep Texaco or any other oil interests out of the Huaorani territory, some international activists fought to save the rainforests while the battle on the local and national level concentrated on protecting the lives and rights of the indigenous peoples. While these two interests did not necessarily compete at all stages of the campaign, at various points in the campaign the differing interests did result in competition. The international campaign against Conoco ran from the late 1980s to the mid 1990s.

In the case against Conoco drilling in Huaorani territory, many U.S. and European based environmental and human rights groups had taken up the issue and staked out political positions which ran the gamut from opposition to Conoco to support for the company as the best option in a bad situation. For the most part, these positions were taken without consultation with the Huaorani (who were deep in the forest) and at best using information provided by a variety of national level actors in Ecuador, but sometimes with no in-country contacts at all. According to one source, the only thing the European and U.S. groups had in common was that the Huaorani people did not recognize any of them.

There was very little flow of information in the campaign between different actors. Strategies were adopted based upon what was considered to be politically feasible, as opposed to what was requested by the affected communities. Deals were agreed to which undercut the rights of indigenous peoples to manage their own territories. In some cases, environmental and human rights organizations raised money in the name of the campaign but did not share those resources in any way with the people on whose behalf they had raised the funds. In fact, activists close to the indigenous people operated on shoe string budgets while those operating in the United States or Europe had lots of money. At one point, a U.S. based environmental organization attempted to cut a deal with Conoco which would have allowed the company to build a road straight through the Huaorani territory. While decisions taken in the international political arena did not immediately jeopardize the safety of thc pcoplc on the ground in Ecuador, those decisions in effect cut off the negotiating abilities of the indigenous communities and destroyed a fledgling alliance between the local arena (indigenous peoples) and the national arena (Ecuadorian environmentalists). The struggle of the Huaorani is still continuing.

The campaign against Conoco in Ecuador provides an example of the worst kind of campaign when measuring political responsibility and accountability.

IDEOLOGY OF NGOS VERSUS RADICAL SOCIO-POLITICAL MOVEMENTS

NGOs emphasize projects not movements; they "mobilize" people to produce at the margins not to struggle to control the basic means of production and wealth; they focus on the technical financial assistance aspects of projects not on structural conditions that shape the everyday lives of people. The NGOs co-opt the language of the Left: "popular power," " empowerment," "gender equality," "sustainable development," "bottom up leadership," etc. The problem is that this language is linked to a framework of collaboration with donors and government agencies that subordinate activity to non-confrontational politics. The local nature of NGO activity means "empowerment" never goes beyond influencing small areas of social life with limited resources within the conditions permitted by the neo-liberal state and macro-economy.

The NGOs and their professional staff directly compete

with the socio-political movements for influence among the poor, women, racially excluded, etc. Their ideology and practice diverts attention from the sources and solutions of poverty (looking downward and inward instead of upward and outward). To speak of micro-enterprises instead of the exploitation by the overseas banks, as solutions to poverty is based on the false notion that the problem is one of individual initiative rather than the transference of income overseas.

The NGOs "aid" affects small sectors of the population, setting up competition between communities for scarce resources and generating insidious distinction and inter and intra community rivalries thus undermining class solidarity. The same is true among the professionals: each sets up their NGO to solicit overseas funds. They compete by presenting proposals closer to the liking of the overseas donors for lower prices, while claiming to speak for more followers. The net effect is a proliferation of NGOs that fragment poor communities into sectoral and sub-sectoral groupings unable to see the larger social picture that afflicts them and even less able to unite in struggle against the system.

Recent experience also demonstrates that foreign donors finance projects during "crises" - political and social challenges to the status quo. Once the movements have ebbed, they shift funding to NGO - regime "collaboration," fitting the NGO projects into the neo-liberal agenda. Economic development compatible with the "free market" rather than social organization for social change becomes the dominant item on the funding agenda.

The structure and nature of NGOs with their "apolitical" posture and their focus on self-help depoliticizes and demobilizes the poor. They reinforce the electoral processes encouraged by the neo-liberal parties and mass media. Political education about the nature of imperialism, the class basis of neo-liberalism, the class struggle between exporters and temporary workers are avoided. Instead the NGOs discuss "the excluded," the "powerless," "extreme poverty," "gender or racial discrimination," without moving beyond the superficial symptom, to engage the social system that produces these conditions. Incorporating the poor into the neo-liberal economy through purely "private voluntary action" the NGOs create a political world where the appearance of solidarity and social action cloaks a conservative conformity with the international and national structure of power.

It is no coincidence that as NGOs have become dominant in certain regions, independent class political action has declined, and neo-liberalism goes uncontested. The bottom line is that the growth of NGOs coincides with increased funding from neo-liberalism and the deepening of poverty everywhere. Despite its claims of many local successes, the overall power of neo-liberalism stands unchallenged and the NGOs increasingly search for niches in the interstices of power.

The problem of formulating alternatives has been hindered in another way. Many of the former leaders of guerrilla and social movements, trade union and popular women's organizations have been co-opted by the NGOs. The offer is tempting: higher pay (occasionally in hard currency), prestige and recognition by overseas donors, overseas conferences and networks, office staff and relative security from repression. In contrast, the socio-political movements offer few material benefits but greater respect and independence and more importantly the freedom to challenge the political and economic system. The NGOs and their overseas banking supporters (Inter-American Bank, the Asian Development Bank, the World Bank) publish newsletters featuring success stories of micro-enterprises and other self-help projects-without mentioning the high rates of failure as popular consumption declines, low price imports flood the market and as interest rates spiral - as is the case in Brazil and Indonesia today.

Even the "successes" affect only a small fraction of the total poor and succeed only to the degree that others cannot enter into the same market. The propaganda value of individual micro-enterprise success, however is important in fostering the illusion that neo-liberalism is a popular phenomenon. The frequent violent mass outbursts that take place in regions of micro-enterprise promotion suggests that the ideology is not hegemonic and the NGOs have not yet displaced independent class movements.

NGO ideology depends heavily on essentialist identity politics, engaging in a rather dishonest polemic with radical movements based on class analysis. They start from the false assumption that class analysis is "reductionist" overlooking the extensive debates and discussions within Marxism on issues of race, ethnicity and gender equality and avoiding the more serious criticism that identities themselves are clearly and profoundly divided by class differences. Take for example, the Chilean or Indian feminist living in a plush suburb drawing a salary 15-20 times that of her domestic servant who works 6 1/2 days a week. Class differences within gender determine housing, living standards, health, educational opportunities and who appropriates who's surplus value. Yet the great majority of NGOs operate on the basis of identity politics and argue that this is the basic point of departure for the new (post-modern politics). Identity politics does not challenge the male dominated elite world of IMF privatizations, multi-national corporations and local landlords.

Rather, it focuses on "patriarchy" in the household, family violence, divorce, family planning, etc. In other words, it fights for gender equality within the micro-world of exploited peoples in which the exploited and impoverished male worker/peasant emerges as the main villain. While no one should support gender exploitation or discrimination at any level, the feminist NGOs do a gross disservice to working women by subordinating them to the greater exploitation of sweatshops which benefit upper class men and women, rent collecting male and female landlords and CEOs of both sexes. The reason the feminist NGOs ignore the "Big Picture" and focus on local issues and personal politics is because billions of dollars flow annually in that direction. If feminist NGOs began to engage in land occupations with men and women landless workers in Brazil or Indonesia or Thailand or the Philippines, if they joined in general strikes of mainly female low-paid rural school teachers against structural adjustment policies, the NGO spigot would get turned off-by their imperial donors. Better to beat up on the local patriarch scratching out an existence in an isolated village in Luzon.

3

NGO Accountability and Sustainable Development

There is little consensus on how to define and classify nongovernmental organisations (NGOs) (Vakil, 1997). The diversity of NGOs strains any simple definition. Hudson (1999) in (O'Dwyer and Unerman, 2008) also supports this diversity in definition and classification by claiming that NGOs cover a huge range of institutions encompassing multinational corporations, voluntary associations, credit unions, farmer's cooperatives, consumer groups, religious organisations, and trade unions.

Wikipedia, the free encyclopedia defines 'Non-governmental organization (NGO) as a term that has become widely accepted as referring to a legally constituted non-governmental organization created by natural or legal persons with no participation or representation of any government'. It goes further to state that 'In the case in which NGOs are funded totally or partially by governments, the NGO maintains its non-governmental status and excludes government representatives from membership in the organization'. Unlike the term intergovernmental organization, "non-governmental organization" is a term in general use but is not a legal definition. In many jurisdictions these types of organizations are defined as "civil society organizations" or referred to by other names (Wikipedia).

Despite lack of consensus in the definition and classification of NGOs, their vision and mission are not in doubt. In the course of the 20th Century and since the era of globalization, NGOs have become so important contributing significantly to humanitarian issues, developmental aid and sustainable development. Thus, failure of governments and challenge of development have led to the multiplicity of NGOs.

Non-governmental organizations (NGOs) are organizations with good and noble intentions to serve public interest. Alternative terms used to describe NGOs include; independent sector, volunteer sector, civil society, grassroots organizations, quasi-autonomous non-governmental organizations, transnational social movement organizations, private voluntary organizations, self-help organizations technical assistance NGOs and non-state actors (NSA's) Perhaps one classification that could be useful for the purpose and dimension of NGO transparency and accountability is that provided by the World Bank which divides them into Operational and Advocacy.

"The diversity of NGOs strains any simple definition. They include many groups and institutions that are entirely or largely independent of government and that have primarily humanitarian or cooperative rather than commercial objectives. They are private agencies in industrial countries that support international development; indigenous groups organized regionally or nationally; and member-groups in villages. NGOs include charitable and religious associations that mobilize private funds for development, distribute food and family planning services and promote community organization. They also include independent cooperatives, community associations, water-user societies, women's groups and pastoral associations. Citizen Groups that raise awareness and influence policy are also NGOs" (The World Bank, 1990)

The World Bank classifies: *operational* NGOs-whose primary purpose is the design and implementation of development-related projects, and; *advocacy* NGOs-whose primary purpose is to defend or promote a specific cause and who seek to influence the policies and practices of the Bank. This classification is contextual and seeks to enhance collaboration between the Bank and NGOs (The World Bank website) O'Dwyer(2007) sees the work of NGOs' to include being advocates of specific causes such as human rights and social justice, provision of relief and humanitarian assistance, or as being facilitators of development. For the purpose of this study, the classification suggested by (Vakil,1997) which states that NGOs can be distinguished by their essential organisational attributes is employed in the choice of the two NGOs. The first NGO, Growing Businesses Foundation (GBF) is a national NGO which focuses on economic development and empowerment of business organizations at the grassroots level; while the second, Junior Achievement(JA) is an international organisation with focus on development education. The reason for the choice of these NGOs for investigation is due to the role education and small enterprise empowerment and development play in developing nations social and economic lives. The exponential growth in the number of NGOs (O'Dwyer, 2007) since 1990 and their lack of commonality beyond the label 'NGO'(Gray, Bebbington and Collison, 2006) make studies on NGOs (including their accountability) to be situational and contextual. Gray et al (2006) also opine that the sheer range of NGOs eludes definition, hence complicating simple specifications of their accountability. O'Dwyer(2007) argues that NGOs who undertake advocacy on issues surrounding human welfare, rights and development have a central concern for the social element of sustainability or social justice. This is a strong argument that makes studies on NGO accountability unassailable in spite of the complexity surrounding it.

Whatever the classification of NGO and its basis, there has been increased visibility of NGOs and their fulfilment of functions in areas which tend to be neglected by the private and public sectors. NGOs have however been subjected to pressure and criticism to be more transparent and accountable. O'Dwyer(2007) citing states that until the early 1990s, NGOs were not subjected to intense scrutiny regarding their accountability, governance, legitimacy or wide social impacts. The myth of infallibility surrounding them then has since fizzled out. The increasing need for NGOs' accountability is to mitigate the crisis of sustainability and relevance that plague NGOs globally and Nigeria in particular. It is against this background that this paper empirically investigates what form and for whom NGO Accountability is practised in two selected NGOs in Nigeria. This is with a view to enhancing the sustainability of the NGOs and providing a basis for delivering their mandates.

What follows in this paper is organised as follows: The next section provides the dimensions of NGO accountability. This is followed by a literature review on NGO accountability. Research design and methodology is discussed thereafter followed by results and discussion. The final section is the conclusion.

DIMENSIONS OF NGO ACCOUNTABILITY

Prior to the Global Accountability Project (GAP) of (One World Trust, 2006) which added *complaint and grievance mechanism* to the discussion about NGO accountability, attention had been focused on *transparency, legitimacy* and *performance*.Songco (2007) claims that the question of transparency came at a time when massive public and private funds are known to be flowing towards this sector, sometimes in competition with funds that were traditionally going directly to government. Edwards and Hulme (1998) in Songco (2007) recorded that the proportion of total aid from Organisation for Economic Cooperation and Development (OECD) member countries channelled through NGOs rose from 0.7percent in 1975 to 3.6percent in 1985, and at least 5percent in 1993-94 – some US$2.3 billion in absolute terms. This growing trend in funding should engender NGO accountability to external actors and standards, as well as provide a moral basis for internal accountability.

In Nigeria, a number of NGOs have been reported in the various communication media as not been insulated from lack of transparency and corruption that has plagued the country over a number of years. The challenge of lack of accountability and poor transparency in many aspects of the Nigerian economy is very daunting. NGOs CEO have also not been unscathed by huge remunerations, financial scandals and corporate governance issues (Jordan 2005 and Bothwell 2004). Accountability and transparency issues have been the bane of many NGOs especially the small unstructured ones that lack capacity and depth to deliver their mandate.

When a gap exists between the value systems of organisations and their interacting constituencies, then the organisation may face the challenges of legitimacy. Slim (2002) in Songco (2007) frames the NGO legitimacy controversy by challenging NGOs to declare whether they speak as *poor, with the poor, for the poor or simply about the poor.* Or is their action merely a façade and pretentious to execute personal agenda different from the identified group and objectives they purport to serve. Legitimacy is earned not forced.

Jordan(2005) claims that NGO accountability and performance has to do with quality versus the quantity of NGO services. A distinction is made between short-term functional accountability (accounting for resources, use and immediate impacts) and strategic accountability (accounting for the impacts that an NGO's actions have on other organisations and the wider environment). O'Dwyer(2007) also reiterates broader conceptions of and motives for NGO accountability which makes performance measures not limited to their stewardship or proper use of financial resources but to include impacts on 'clients',

The fourth element of accountability which is complaint and grievance mechanisms are "mechanisms through which an organization enables stakeholders to address complaints against its decisions and actions, and through which it ensures that these complaints are properly *reviewed and acted upon".* This enhances stakeholder engagement and wider democratization-an internal driver of NGO accountability (Sustainability, 2003)

The highlighted dimensions of accountability provide a framework over which NGOs should benchmark the attainment or lack of it of their mandate, vision and mission. These dimensions of NGO accountability with their implication on the moral basis of the existence of the NGOs and their wider societal impact form the bases on which the selected NGOs' accountability were evaluated.

Literature Review

Srinivas(2005) claims that NGO accountability covers issues such as organizational management, project implementation, financial management and information disclosure. It is related to issues such as answerability, responsibility, liability, dependability, conscientiousness, reliability, trustworthiness, legitimacy, and transparency. Srinivas(2005) further opines that there has been a rising visibility and stakes of NGOs' work. A crisis of legitimacy in many sectors, especially business and government has amplified the need for NGOs as a 'counterbalance'. More vocal advocacy by NGOs has also challenged the work of corporations, governments and international organizations, which in turn has elicited counterattacks. Their potential to address institutional failures (formal and/or informal) for global problems is also being increasingly recognized. On the other hand, Srinivas(2005) concludes that cases of NGO misconduct in advocacy, fund use, management, and governance, have come to light, questioning their very legitimacy and congruency with social values and expectations. Some NGO have also ignored the fact that they are answerable to key stakeholders and the constituency that they work with, for promises of performance.

The complexity of NGO accountability was enunciated

by Lloyd and de las Casas(2005) being due to the need to be accountable to many different sets of stakeholders which, separately and collectively, play an integral part in their operations:

- institutional donors provide funding;
- governments provide legal and regulatory frameworks;
- supporters provide their money and time;
- beneficiaries provide the basis for an organization's purpose and moral legitimacy.

Possible explanation for the focus on NGOs accountability and responses in that direction is not unconnected with NGOs desire to create, maintain or repair their societal legitimacy. Arguably, legitimacy theory, a theory applied in social and environmental accounting is a plausible explanation for NGO accountability. Other theories that provide a sound theoretical foundation to substantiate the value of NGO accountability include Stakeholder theory; Institutional theory and Resource Dependence theory

Legitimacy theory (Lindblom, 1994; Suchman, 1995) is value system centred. A dichotomy exists between the value system of organisations and those of the society. Legitimacy exists at the organisational level when there is congruence between organisation and society value system. Legitimacy refers to perceptions by key stakeholders that the existence, activities and impacts of Civil Society Organisations (CSOs) are justifiable and appropriate in terms of central social values and institutions. Legitimacy is grounded in the perceptions of stakeholders in the larger environment in which the organization is embedded. It is about an organization fulfilling its social contract with the society. Legitimacy is the right to be and do something in society-a sense that an organization is lawful, admissible, and justified in its chosen course of action (Edwards, 2000). An NGO legitimacy could be official, democratic, or earned through value added.

Institutional theory, unlike legitimacy theory specifies how society expectations are met and gained by institutionalising norms and rules. Institutional theory attends to the deeper and more resilient aspects of social structure. It considers the processes by which structures, including schemas, rules, norms, and routines, become established as authoritative guidelines for social behaviour. It inquires into how these elements are created, diffused, adopted, and adapted over space and time; and how they fall into decline and disuse. Although the ostensible subject is stability and order in social life, students of institutions must perforce attend not just to consensus and conformity but to conflict and change in social structures (Scott, 2004). This theory provides some code of behaviour to earn, nurture and maintain societal expectations; and thus create a positive organisation-society interface.

Resource dependence theory concerns itself with the strategy organisations adopt in drawing resources from the environment. This position is imperative because organisations are interdependent with selves and the environment. The resolution by organisations of different and conflicting expectations of different stakeholders is what stakeholder theory engages in. This is more necessary because of divergent impacts different stakeholders have on organisations. In spite of the diversity in their level of analysis and specificity, the various theories are united in their resolve to advance and sustain positive organisation – society interface. Various authors, accounting associations, researchers, donors, governments, corporations, and international agencies raise important questions about the issue of NGO accountability and concluded (based on different objectives) that NGO accountability is important to both the internal and external users. Accountability also contributes to the effectiveness of NGO work and the legitimacy of their advocacy.

Bendell (2006) concluded based on the submissions of eleven world leading NGOs that the core values and operating principles for international NGOs, should include good governance and management; fundraising and multi-stakeholder engagement. It also makes specific reference to respect for universal principles (such as the Universal Declaration of Human Rights), independence, responsible advocacy, effective programmes, non-discrimination, transparency and ethical fundraising.

With regard to the evolution of NGO accountability practices and their implications on NGOs, Songco (2007) finds that the effort of creating a more proactive environment for NGO accountability is to dissect the different levels at which accountability needs to be promoted, the methods that can be used by NGOs operating in these different levels and incentives and disincentives that can be instituted in this regard.

Lloyd R. and de las Casas, L. (2005) investigate NGO self-regulation and its impact on enforcing and balancing accountability. They argue that increasing visibility and increasing criticism, among other factors, have led to growing pressure on NGOs to be more accountable both from within and outside of the sector. One increasingly prominent means, they said, of doing so is self regulation, but without means of enforcement how effective is this? And how can self-policing codes tilt the balance in accountability procedures away from the powerful (donors and governments) and towards the NGO's beneficiaries – those people on whose behalf an NGO claims to be working and who, after all, provide the rationale for its existence.

Drawing on the theoretical constructs of hierarchical and holistic accountability9, O'Dwyer and Unerman (2008) investigate developments in accountability practices at the Irish section of the human rights advocacy NGO Amnesty International and find that while managers favoured the development of holistic accountability mechanisms exhibiting accountability to a wide range of stakeholders, a hierarchical conception of accountability privileging a narrow range of (potentially) powerful stakeholders, has begun to dominate external accountability discourse and practice.

This paper also draws on the work of (Ebrahim,2003) which recognizes five broad mechanisms for NGOs accountability in practice: reports and disclosure statements, performance assessments and evaluations, participation, self-regulation, and social audits. Ebrahim (2003) analysed these five mechanisms along three dimensions of accountability: upward-downward, internal-external, and functional-strategic; and observed that accountability in practice has emphasized upward and external accountability to donors while downward and internal mechanisms remain comparatively underdeveloped. Moreover, NGOs and funders have focused primarily on shortterm 'functional' accountability responses at the expense of longer-term 'strategic' processes necessary for lasting social and political change.

Research Design and Methodology.

Case study method approach was employed in carrying out the study. We selected two NGOs (one indigenous and the other with foreign affiliation) representing respectively SME development and Education thematic areas. The available Data on NGO accountability for the selected case studies were elicited from the managers and accountants through interview process. The information obtained from the interview was corroborated with content review of annual account and reports, and also the websites of the NGOs. The nature of the questions during the interview, the content review of the annual report and account, and the websites were with a view to determining for whom, on what, and for what purpose NGO accountability was premised on. Specifically, it was investigated whether accountability was based on self regulation: internal or external accountability, financial or nonfinancial. It was also investigated whether accountability was top down or bottom up; whether accountability was from the hierarchical or holistic perspective. We also investigated whether they were subjected to regulatory control, maintenance of code of conduct and observance of standards. The five broad mechanisms for NGOs accountability in practice(Ebrahim,2003): reports and disclosure statements, performance assessments and evaluations, participation, selfregulation, and social audits were borne in mind in drafting the interview questions. We were also on the look out for the dimensions of the accountability practiced by these NGOs along the line suggested by (Ebrahim,2003): upward-downward, internal-external, and functional-strategic

4

A Survey of the Debate on NGO Accountability

Because NGOs have been internationally active for over two centuries (Charnovitz, 1997), there are many historical episodes one could use as a springboard into a discussion of NGO accountability. Yet, before NGO influence is strong enough on a global scale to spark demands for accountability, such activist NGOs must exist. Therefore, an appropriate place to start will be an authoritative statement articulating the legitimacy of NGOs. The 1891 Encyclical of Pope Leo XIII on Capital and Labour, which had an important influence on the development of liberal regimes to oversee labour unions (Pope Leo XIII, 1891). The Encyclical contrasts 'civil society' with the 'lesser societies', and indicates that the latter, the private associations, 'are now far more common than before'. The Encyclical offers 'cheering hope for the future provided always that the associations We have described continue to grow and spread, and are well and wisely administered'. The societies described in the Encyclical are societies of working men, employers and benevolent foundations.

Entering into such societies is 'the natural right of man'. Thus, the Encyclical explains that for a state to forbid its citizens to form associations contradicts the very principle of the state's existence, namely, to protect natural rights. The Pope concedes that the law should intervene to prevent certain bad associations, but counsels that 'every precaution should be taken not to violate the rights of individuals and not to impose unreasonable regulations under pretense of public benefit'. Moreover, the state 'should not thrust itself into their [the associations'] peculiar concerns and their organization, for things move and live by the spirit inspiring them, and may be killed by the rough grasp of a hand from without'. The Encyclical provides a philosophical underpinning for relaxed state regulation of NGOs.

The term 'non-governmental organization' came into use at least as early as 1920. In that year, Sophy Sanger employed the term in a discussion of how such organizations had not been able to participate in the first multilateral negotiations for labour treaties in 1906 (Sanger, 1920). Sanger contrasted this pre-war practice to the advent of the International Labour Organization (ILO) in 1919. The constitutional provisions of the ILO set out in the Treaty of Versailles call for the participation of 'non-Government Delegates and advisers chosen in agreement with the industrial organisations, if such organisations exist, which are the most representative of employers or workpeople, as the case may be, in their respective countries'. In the ILO, each member state sends four delegates-two from government, one employer and one worker. The employers and workers are not members of the ILO, however, because only nation-states are members. A question regarding the representativeness of the ILO worker delegate from The Netherlands arose during the third session of the International Labour Conference (1921) when the Dutch Government's choice was contested by the Netherlands Confederation of Trade Unions. The ILO Conference extended the credential to the delegate chosen by the Dutch Government, but asked the ILO Governing Body to request the Council of the League of Nations to seek an advisory opinion from the Permanent Court of International Justice (PCIJ). This disagreement became the first matter to come before and be decided by the PCIJ. In 1922, the PCIJ held that The Netherlands had not violated the Treaty of Versailles in making its selection. In considering the matter before it, the PCIJ welcomed oral statements from the International Labour Office and two international labour union federations.

The openness of the PCIJ to statements by NGOs was an important episode in the history of NGO roles in international law. If an NGO-related question were to come to the International Court of Justice (ICJ) today, that Court would not allow NGOs to submit their own statements. No NGO participation in the ICJ has occurred since it was established in 1946, and the last requests by NGOs for an opportunity to submit amicus briefs in noncontentious cases were denied (Shelton, 1994). The ICJ may be the only international arena in which NGOs have lost participatory opportunities since the 1920s.

The ILO Constitution is unusual in positing that the non-governmental delegates are to be 'representative' of specified constituencies within a country. Typically, the constitutions of international organizations that provide for NGO participation do not call for a representative body or suggest that the role of the NGO is to represent anyone in particular. For example, Article 71 of the United Nations (UN) Charter states that: 'The Economic and

Social Council may make suitable arrangements for consultation with non-governmental organizations which are concerned with matters within its competence'. Thus, the stated rationale for NGO consultation is the concern of the NGO rather than the breadth of its membership or its representativeness.

Nevertheless, when it implemented Article 71 in 1950, the UN Economic and Social Council (ECOSOC) formulated a set of principles providing that the consulted organization 'shall be of recognized standing and shall represent a substantial portion of the organized persons within the particular field in which it operates'. This requirement, to some extent, has been carried forward into the current ECOSOC Credentialing Arrangements, adopted in 1996. These Arrangements state that the NGO 'shall be of recognized standing within the particular field of its competence or of a representative character'.

The Arrangements also state that: 'The organization shall have a representative structure and possess appropriate mechanisms of accountability to its members, who shall exercise effective control over its policies and actions through the exercise of voting rights or other appropriate democratic and transparent decision-making processes'. Although most of the international legal agreements that provide for public participation in international organizations extend that participation to NGOs rather than to individuals, one prominent exception is the World Bank Inspection Panel that permits requests for inspection from 'any group of two or more people in the country where the Bank-financed project is located who believe that as a result of the Bank's violation their rights or interests have been, or are likely to be, adversely affected in a direct and material way'. The Inspection Panel is a good example of a clear accountability mechanism for an international organization because the Panel reviews whether the Bank's actions are consistent with a prescribed set of standards-in this case, the Bank's own rules.

INTERNATIONAL LAW AND POLITICS

A voluminous literature exists on the accountability (or lack thereof) of NGOs. Those writing on NGO accountability include lawyers, political scientists, economists, journalists and others. Some of the studies discussed below mix the issues of legitimacy, democratic accountability and plain accountability. Starting with some opinion-shapers, in 2003 The New York Times (21 July) editorialized that: 'non-governmental organizations are now part of the power structure too'. They receive donations from the public and advocate policies that each group claims are in the public interest. As they become part of the established political landscape worldwide, 'these groups owe it to the public to be accountable and transparent themselves' (The New York Times, 21 July 2003). Pursuing a similar theme shortly afterwards, The Economist ran an influential essay 'Who Guards the Guardians?', which put forth the 'novel idea' of 'auditing NGOs' (The Economist, 20 September 2003). More so than any other general interest journal, The Economist has been attentive to the phenomenon of NGOs. In 2000, The Economist asserted that NGOs 'can get into bad ways because they are not accountable to anyone' (29 January 2000).

Perhaps the most critical perspective on NGOs comes from John Bolton. Writing in 2000 before he joined the Bush Administration, Bolton expressed concern about the 'extra-national clout of NGOs' in global governance and worried that 'Civil society also sees itself as beyond national politics, which is one of the reasons its recent successes have such profoundly anti-democratic implications' (Bolton, 2000).

The problem, as analysed by Bolton, is that NGO participation 'provides a second opportunity for intrastate advocates to reargue their positions, thus advantaging them over their opponents who are either unwilling or unable to reargue their cases in international fora'. Moreover, he contended that 'the civil society idea actually suggests a "corporative" approach to international decision-making that is dramatically troubling for democratic philosophy because it posits "interests" (whether NGOs or businesses) as legitimate actors along with popularly elected governments'. Bolton, who is known for speaking his mind, went even further to claim that such corporativism is synonymous with fascism and that 'Mussolini would smile on the Forum of Civil Society' while 'Americanists would not'.

Yet this assertion by Bolton elides the fact that the Italian dictator and the fascist movement were seeking to control associations and to suppress any independence from the state (Tannenbaum, 1969). Bolton does not advocate suppressing NGOs, but he seems to want a government to shut its eyes to them. Bolton's article fails to explain why he thinks that 'Americanists' (a term he does not define) should not smile on a Forum of Civil Society. No other published criticism rivals Bolton's venom towards NGOs. All of the studies discussed hereafter offer criticisms of the NGO role within an analytical framework that accepts the legitimacy of voluntary, independent associations.

Several years ago, Kenneth Anderson wrote an article

about the efforts by NGOs during negotiations for the treaty on landmines and he used that case study to offer more general observations on the NGO role (Anderson, 2000). Anderson's article made an important contribution to the international law scholarship on NGOs. Anderson calls attention to the development of a 'romance', 'partnership' or 'symbiotic' relationship between international NGOs, sympathetic states and international organizations. Anderson objects to this relationship because, in his view, 'international NGOs' are not conduits from the 'people' and do not operate from the bottom up. Rather, he says, 'the glory of organizations of civil society is not democratic legitimacy, but the ability to be a pressure group' that will speak horizontally to other global elites. Such a horizontal conversation has a 'worthwhile, essential function in making the world-sometimes at least, a better place-but it does not reduce the democratic deficit' (Anderson, 2000).

These observations by Anderson about the NGO role show considerable insight and balance, but in more recent scholarship, Anderson seems to have lost that balance (Anderson, 2001). In offering advice to the Bush Administration, Anderson warns against a 'pragmatic conservative model' that would not oppose NGOs, but rather would merely seek 'to temper their extreme impulses and encourage them towards sensible actions and advocacy positions'. Instead, Anderson argues that stronger policies are needed because there are 'risks to democracy' from the activities of international NGOs. These risks ensue because there is a difference between NGOs operating domestically in a democratic society and NGOs operating in the international field. The alleged difference is that the NGOs do their domestic lobbying within a democratic structure, but that 'in the undemocratic international world' matters are different because the 'international system... has no democratic legitimacy'.

The degree of legitimacy declined after the international system began 'embarking on the path of downgrading democratic sovereigns and upgrading the supposed legitimacy of international NGOs'. Anderson (2001) points to two specific harms from NGOs. First, 'international NGOs muddy the waters of the critical question of how much power ought to be assigned to a system of international organizations that cannot ever be democratic'. Second, 'international NGOs actively seek to undermine the processes of democracy within democratic states whenever the results of those democratic processes produce, in the view of the international NGOs, uncongenial substantive outcomes'. As a result, he says, one should regard 'international NGOs, unlike their domestic counterparts-or unlike the international NGOs themselves when they work within sovereign democratic systems-as not merely undemocratic, but as profoundly antidemocratic'. Furthermore he asserts that international NGOs have felt themselves on the defensive with respect to the fundamental question asked by David Rieff (1999), namely, 'So who elected the NGOs?'.

A number of unanswered questions leap out of Anderson's analysis. One is what is the difference between the criticized NGO activity of seeking to undermine or reverse the decisions taken by a democratic state and the uncriticized activity of NGOs working within the domestic political system to undermine official decisions? Why does Anderson think that the situs of NGO advocacy changes its democratic character? Another question is why could it be antidemocratic for international NGOs to focus their advocacy efforts on the decisions being made by and within international organizations? The international organizations are undemocratic or cannot ever be democratic, but even if international organizations are undemocratic today, how can the NGO voice reduce the level of legitimacy since ultimately it is up to sovereigns to decide whether to follow any of the advice being offered by the NGOs? Another puzzle in Anderson's analysis is how NGOs could pose 'risks to democracy when international NGOs propose themselves as substitutes for democracy' if, as he believes, there is no democracy at risk anyway in the realm of international organizations?

If Anderson's point is that NGOs pose risks to national democracy when they lobby in UN meetings, then he does not explain what that risk is. Martha Schweitz offers a more positive view on the question of whether NGO participation in world governance is legitimate. She explains that the issue is not the legitimacy of a claim to obedience, but rather the legitimacy of participation by NGOs in distinct roles in the international governance process. A key myth to dispel, she proclaims, is 'the myth that NGOs must be representative organizations in order to be legitimate participants'.

She explains that NGOs have at least three reasons for being that have nothing to do with representing anyone in particular: first, being sources of information and expertise; second, delivering services to people; and third, standing up for a core value. In her view, there is no minimum threshold for the number of people in the world that need to share a value for it to be heard in the international arena. Schweitz also addresses whether there should be some 'standards of conduct' pertaining to certain NGO roles and suggests that 'We need to think about what makes an NGO a good world citizen'.

Gary Johns (2000) raises concerns about some of the assumptions underlying the NGO accountability movement. Johns argues that when NGOs posit that they are a new form of democratic legitimacy or the greatest expression of democracy, then NGOs may become subject to 'a policy of heavy-handed regulation of private associations'. Johns sees this path as undesirable from a 'liberal' perspective, and suggests that each NGO should 'claim no more than to represent a view' and should not seek to belittle the authority of representative democracy. In his view, the only scrutiny needed for NGOs is 'the ordinary scrutiny of any group or person who seeks to make claims on the public', that is, the 'integrity and truth of the proposal'.

Several analysts point to standards of conduct that NGOs violate or to general accountability problems with NGOs. For example, a decade ago, Julie Mertus warned of the 'dangers of NGOs that violate democratic norms' (Mertus, 1995). She notes that the operations of NGOs 'are at times decidedly opaque', and that the 'institutions of civil society may run against the most basic rule of democracy, namely, to govern with the consent of the governed'.

One conclusion she reaches is that 'As long as international law fails to articulate a clear and consistent position as to the responsibility of non-State actors', these actors may continue to neglect human rights. Jan Aart Scholte, a long-time scholar of 'civil society', observes that even though 'civil society groups have an obligation to answer to stakeholders for their actions and omissions', most of these groups 'have operated very limited and unimaginative accountability mechanisms in relation to their own activities' (Scholte, 2004). He sees such accountability shortfalls as being politically costly to 'civil society' work because authorities seize on missing accountability to reject the legitimacy of those groups in global governance. In contrast, Scholte reports on a number of innovative actions to promote accountability.

For example, the Philippine Council for NGO Certification has developed a rigorous scheme of 'nonofficial oversight for civil society in that country' (Golub in this volume). Peter Spiro (2002) seeks to unpack NGO accountability by asking to whom the accountability should be developed. His answer is that NGOs should be accountable both to their constituencies and to process, and he frames that distinction as internal versus external accountability. Regarding internal accountability to members, he suggests that the problem of accountability is exaggerated because there are practical constraints on NGOs (such as membership) that keep them in line. In evaluating NGO internal accountability, he cautions against the 'fetishization of other forms of association', such as the democratic state, which is 'implicitly idealized on the accountability metric, especially by virtue of periodic elections'. In Spiro's view, voting is a 'crude tool for keeping governmental authorities in line' and 'governments can get away with an awful lot before having to answer to their memberships'.

Regarding external accountability of NGOs to 'the system', Spiro contends that this process now operates sub-optimally because, given the present informal arrangements for NGO participation, NGOs lack incentives to be accountable.

Spiro's proposed solution is for states to accept 'formal inclusion of non-state actors in international decision-making' in order to 'hold NGOs, as repeat players, accountable to international bargains'. Michael Edwards is one of the world's most thoughtful and experienced analysts of NGO activities. Edwards (2000) explains that 'NGO accountability is weak and problematic, since there is no clear "bottom line" for results and no single authority to which NGOs must report on their activities'. Edwards advocates a 'New Deal' in which more participation in global governance is granted 'in return for transparency and accountability on a set of minimum standards for NGO integrity and performance, monitored largely through self-regulation' plus a 'much larger array of voluntary regulations and other, non-coercive means of influencing destructive behaviour'. Greater accountability, in Edwards's view, is needed both upward, to donors, and downward, to the poor. Edwards contributes the useful notion of vertical accountability, namely, that on development issues, the claims made by the large NGOs should be rooted in the experience at the local level. Another constructive suggestion is to foster innovation in global governance through 'a period of structured experimentation in NGO involvement'.

Hugo Slim offers a working definition of NGO accountability, which is 'the process by which an NGO holds itself openly responsible for what it believes, what it does, and what it does not do in a way that shows it involving all concerned parties and actively responding to what it learns' (Slim, 2002). Slim proposes constructing a map of the NGOs' various stakeholders in a given situation because NGO accountability cannot be expected to be uniform across a wide range of NGO activity. The map may reveal conflicting interests and will help in the design of the right accountability mechanisms, such as social audits or a complaint procedure.

Benedict Kingsbury (2002) reflects on NGO accountability as a constitutional challenge. He explains that the struggle to articulate a useful approach to establishing 'rigorous accountability of non-state actors suggests that international civil society has at present minimal conceptual resources other than First Amendment liberalism for structuring thought about problems of accountability'. Yet First Amendment liberalism, according to Kingsbury, offers few means of NGO accountability except via markets, and it tends to view demands for other forms of accountability with suspicion. Moreover, he says, First Amendment liberalism is not very helpful in addressing the participatory claims of ascriptive groups, such as indigenous peoples exercising governmental powers. Kingsbury calls for the development of 'a richer international constitutionalism' to help address accountability, mandate, representation and participation.

An extremely impressive analysis of human rights NGO accountability has recently been authored by Robert Charles Blitt (2004). Blitt takes a selfdescribed law and economics approach to the question of whether human rights NGOs should be regulated in order to enhance their accountability. Blitt refers to human rights NGOs as 'human rights organizations' or HROs. First, in order to make a case for regulation of the HRO industry, there needs to be a problem. The overall problem Blitt sees is that the current market for HRO ideas and activism does not operate in a way so as to assure that the product is safe for those who consume or are affected by it. He suggests that HROs 'shoulder a virtual duty of care to the general public'. Blitt provides a number of reasons to be doubtful that the internal accountability controls on HROs are adequate-for example, he says that NGO reliance on government funding may operate to limit the independence of NGOs or, conversely, cause them to neglect their primary interests in reliability and objectivity.

Then Blitt analyses the potential external controls, such as the media, donors, international organizations and the free market, and finds these controls to be inadequate. He devotes many pages to analysing the marketplace of ideas and argues that like any market, it may need regulation if there are dysfunctions. Among the harms he notes are the damage to an impugned body's reputation from misleading allegations, the futility of seeking judicial relief on small-size transactions and the difficulty of private law remedies because of extra-jurisdictional issues.

Blitt's solution is industry self-regulation, in other words, the major HROs should establish detailed standards for operations, and invite all HROs to subscribe to them voluntarily. The standards would cover: professional staff and board membership criteria; financial and financial disclosure transparency; best practices for research, fact-finding and reporting; and protocols for issuing public retractions. Blitt makes clear that 'governments would have no role to play in setting HRO standards'. Once standards are adopted, they could be monitored and enforced in several ways, such as an independent monitoring agency, annual ratings of HROs, or best practices for financial agreements. He concludes that 'while individuals may remain free to establish fly-by-night HROs, recognized HROs will have an authoritative and objective tool that can be harnessed to credential themselves in the eyes of the media, governments, intergovernmental agencies, courts and the public at large' (Blitt, 2004).

NGO accountability is also being addressed in the reports of major international advisory commissions. In June 2004, the Panel of Eminent Persons on United Nations-Civil Society Relations appointed by Secretary-

General Kofi Annan delivered its report and suggested that UN practices for engaging civil society should work to define 'standards of governance, such as those for transparency and accountability' (UN, 2004). In particular, according to the Panel, the UN Secretariat should discuss with the private groups advising the UN 'possible codes of conduct and self-policing mechanisms to heighten disciplines of quality, governance and balance'.

In January 2005, a Consultative Board appointed by the World Trade Organization (WTO) Director-General delivered an extensive report that included a brief section on NGO accountability. The Board noted the criticism that 'those lobbying for more access' are 'often neither especially accountable nor particularly transparent themselves'. Furthermore, the Board intoned: 'While there is now a broad recognition among member states of the UN of the substantial and proven benefits of non-governmental participation in intergovernmental debate on global issues, there are continuing concerns about the legitimacy, representativity, accountability and politics of non-governmental organizations.'

In reaching its conclusion, the Board of eight men neglected to hold any public hearings or to solicit public comments during its investigation, a period that lasted over 18 months.

RECONCEPTUALIZING NGO ACCOUNTABILITY

In their 1959 article in the American Journal of International Law, 'The Identification and Appraisal of Diverse Systems of Public Order', McDougal and Lasswell describe a 'world social process' in which the participants 'are acting individually in their own behalf and in concert with others'. They emphasize that 'The ultimate actor is always the individual human being who may act alone or through any organization', and they talk of associations that 'do not concentrate upon power but primarily seek other values'.

By starting with the individual, McDougal and Lasswell avoid two analytical pitfalls. First, because individuals are seen as active participants, social and power process can be viewed as 'expanding circles of interaction' or as a 'series of arenas ranging in comprehensiveness from the globe as a whole... to nation states, provinces and cities, on down to the humblest village and township'. In this analytical approach, there is no need to explain why individuals should be able to participate at broader (or higher) levels of decision-making, just as they do in narrower (or lower) levels. Second, in positing the expanding circles, McDougal and Lasswell avoid the 'impossible separation of national and transnational law' (Lasswell and McDougal, 1997).

The jurisprudence of human dignity they propose is applicable at all levels. The notion of the individual being governed in a multitude of arenas is empirically convincing and normatively valuable. On any given day, the individual may be confronted with the dictates and decisions of his homeowner community, employer, local government, provincial government, national government and international organizations. The distance between the individual and his homeowner community may be closer than the distance to the UN, but the ability of the individual to influence any of the authoritative decisions may be very limited. Consider, for example, the innocent victims who suffer collateral damage as a result of sanctions ordered by the UN Security Council (Reinisch, 2001), or the individuals dying of fatal illnesses who are being denied potentially effective drug treatments due to the precautionary approach used by the US Food and Drug Administration (Minor, 2005).

The normative value of seeing the individual as the object of simultaneous, multiple levels of lawmaking is that the truth becomes self-evident that an individual will have an interest in influencing all of the authoritative decisions that affect her, including not only those made by officials that she has elected, but also decisions made by others. From the perspective of the individual, the webs of authority enveloping her may be distinct in some ways, but the need to engage in politics is omnipresent. Although the strategies one uses in various political arenas will likely differ, the moral justification for purposive action will be the same-the pursuit of self-fulfilment and a just community order.

When is NGO Accountability Needed?

The literature on NGO accountability features a common thread, which is that internationally active NGOs should be subject to oversight and restraints by accountability holders. When a lens of democratic accountability is placed over NGOs, they can appear to be unaccountable because they are not publicly elected and because of the non-existence of a global public for ongoing validation of NGO actions.

Moreover, the restraints against abuse-fiscal, reputational and legal constraints-may not operate very well for some NGOs. The potential abuses include violating national laws, making false claims that tarnish the reputations of others, engaging in activities that abridge human rights, wasting financial contributions and misapprehending the public interest. In answering, one should start with the individual. What accountability for an individual's actions is expected? We expect the individual to be accountable to her conscience, to her family, to whatever deity she recognizes, to the laws of the governments that have jurisdiction over her, to entities with which she has entered contractual relations (such as employers), and generally to those to whom she has made a commitment. This is an extensive range of accountability, but hardly seems all-encompassing in the sense that an individual is to be accountable to all humans for all of her thoughts and deeds. In other words, my claim is that on a day-to-day basis, the individual engages in many acts of volition that are an exercise of her autonomy and for which no accountability is expected.

Certainly, accountability needs to be in place for physically harmful NGO activities. Whenever an NGO engages in illegal or terrorist activity, then obviously it ought to be accountable to national criminal justice systems or to the UN Security Council. In recent years, the Security Council has often targeted non-state actors with economic sanctions.

Such retaliation against private persons through joint governmental action is not a new development, as multilateral legislation against dangerous organizations began with the Protocol of 1904 against the Anarchist Movement. Mundane illegal activity in NGOs can incur accountability under domestic law. An association committing criminal acts such as financial disruptions or eco-terrorism may be prosecuted (Crimm, 2004). Associations and their employees may also be liable under domestic law for potential torts such as negligence or defamation, and for violations of tax and corporate governance requirements.

A key question underlying the debate about NGO

accountability is whether a new system is needed for oversight of NGOs, and if so, whether it should be formulated as a legal instrument. Ironically, the international organization on the cutting edge of applying international rules to NGOs is the WTO. The WTO has rules regarding public and private organizations that engage in standard-setting on products (that is, goods). These rules appear in the WTO Agreement on Technical Barriers to Trade (TBT), which directs governments to 'take such reasonable measures as may be appropriate to them to ensure that local government and non-governmental standardizing bodies within their territories... accept and comply' with the TBT Code of Good Practice for the Preparation, Adoption and Application of Standards. Among the requirements of the Code are that governmental and non-governmental standardizing bodies shall: first, play a full part in relevant international standardizing bodies with participation, whenever possible, taking place through one delegation representing all standardizing bodies in the territory; second, make every effort to achieve a national consensus on the standards to be developed; third, publish a work programme at least once every six months; fourth, before adopting a standard, allow a period of at least 60 days for the submission of comments by interested parties within the territory of that Member; fifth, take any submitted comments into account and, if so requested, reply to them as promptly as possible; and sixth, make an objective effort to resolve any complaints submitted by other standardizing bodies that have accepted the Code.

Although the term 'accountability' is not used, the WTO TBT Code contains limited accountability norms of representation, consensus building, transparency, addressing complaints and giving a reply. The supervision of NGO operations through the TBT Agreement is a little-noticed phenomenon in WTO law. While there is nothing substantively wrong with the norms being demanded of standardizing organizations, some dissonance exists because the WTO itself does not practice what it preaches. The internal procedures of WTO committees do not provide for a public notice and comment period for WTO rule-making, and governments at the WTO can take positions without showing that their view is backed by a national consensus.

The WTO has increased the power of public and private international standard-setting bodies that devise international standards because such standards are now enforceable through the WTO. Under TBT rules, WTO member governments must use international standards where they exist as a basis for the government's own technical regulations. Because a national government can be required to follow international standards even when it disagrees with them, governments may want to assure that national interests are well represented by the national organization that serves on the international body. Typically, the national organization is an NGO. A little-known US law, enacted in 1979, addresses this situation and provides authority to the Secretary of Commerce to oversee the adequacy of the 'representation' of US interests in standard-setting, and if necessary, to take steps to provide for adequate representation. To my knowledge, no use has been made of this important administrative mechanism.

Beyond specialized WTO rules, no other multilateral discipline exists for NGO accountability. Should there be? Because NGO activity is multifarious, the answer to this question has to be highly textured. For operational activities by NGOs (for example, immunizations), one might demand more accountability than for advocacy by NGOs. For some operational activities, NGOs act as contractors. When NGOs are in a principal-agent relationship, certainly the NGO should be accountable to the principal. Yet much of NGO activity in world politics does not fit that typology because it lacks an external principal, and thus there is no ability to account to anybody. For NGOs, the key relationship is membership. The individual joins the NGO and puts time, money, voice and loyalty into it, and at some point exits the NGO.

Peter Spiro's (2002) distinction between internal and external accountability is a useful place to begin an analysis. When NGOs are in a corporate form, various internal governance obligations (in national law) ensue, such as accountability of the executives of the NGO to its trustees, accountability of employees to management and restraints against financial self-dealing. To enhance internal (and external accountability), governments often impose reporting and transparency requirements on NGOs. The UN has demanded that an NGO in consultative status 'possess appropriate mechanisms of accountability to its members'. Stronger internal accountability can be responsive to the concern that NGOs are totally unchaperoned and are not accountable to anyone.

With respect to external accountability, funding agencies and foundations are likely to demand and obtain some degree of accountability (Ovsiovitch, 1998; Pettit, forthcoming). Sometimes in an NGO, there may be tension between accountability to the foundation giving it financial support and allegiance to the intended beneficiaries who may see the world differently than the foundation's grant officer. The most difficult issue regarding external accountability is the extent to which an NGO needs to be explicitly accountable to 'the public', or to the class of beneficiaries that the NGO purports to aid. When analysts criticize NGO activity, the criticism often takes the form that the NGO is not serving the cause it claims to serve. Assuming that such a problem exists, how can we address it through more intelligently designed accountability systems?

A key design consideration will be that if the concern is external global accountability of NGOs, then the optimal system may need to be transnational. When legal measures are used, some harmonization of law or mutual recognition should be considered so that NGOs operating globally are not subjected to conflicting domestic laws. When market or voluntary measures are used, there will be challenges of identifying the relevant stakeholders and sorting out inconsistent preferences among the stakeholders. For example, suppose an NGO in one country wants to preserve the wildlife in another, and yet the residents of the second country prefer development over preservation. In that situation, no unambiguous measure of NGO accountability seems to exist.

With so many different kinds of NGO activity in global governance, one promising approach is to distinguish various pieces. Consider a distinction between: first, delegated responsibilities; second, assumed responsibilities; and third, advocacy.

1 Delegated responsibilities occur when the international community delegates a task to an NGO. For example, the UN Security Council occasionally requests NGOs to provide assistance. The Red Cross organizations are authorized and expected to perform various humanitarian functions. NGOs are used to certify vessel compliance with international rules regarding

pollution from ships and safety of life at sea (Murphy, 2005). Although not exactly a delegated function, it is interesting to note that in June 2004, two NGOs were invited by the UN Security Council to give a briefing to the Council, meeting in regular session, regarding the role of civil society in post-conflict peace building.

2 Assumed responsibilities occur when an NGO takes on a needed task that no one else is doing adequately. For example, Rotary International has launched a project to eradicate polio. Another example is election monitoring, which has been greatly facilitated by NGOs. In the same way, the international regime to protect endangered species benefits immeasurably from constant monitoring by TRAFFIC, a joint program of the World Wildlife Fund and IUCN (The World Conservation Union).

3 Advocacy is the NGO's use of its voice to influence world policy-making within international organizations and in national capitals. Just about every issue today experiences NGO advocacy. The nature of an accountability system should vary depending on what is being carried out.

The significance of making a person (a natural person or NGO) accountable is that the person owes a duty to a single or discrete set of accountability holders. For many NGO activities that duty exists, but for many others it does not. To suggest that an NGO should be accountable to the 'general public' or to the 'system' is doubly wrong-first, because drawing such dotted lines of accountability to the public itself is not feasible, and second and more importantly, because the general public is not the accountability holder of a free association of individuals.

This is particularly so when the NGO activity at issue is the expression of ideas. The fact that NGOs may use their voice to call for intergovernmental organizations to be more accountable to the public does not provide a reason to turn the tables on the NGO and demand it to be equally accountable to the public. A similar problem would ensue in trying to make NGOs 'accountable' to beneficiaries. The real problem with NGOs is not that they are unaccountable, but rather that they suffer in various degrees from poor management and poor performance. Such behaviour often leads people to say that NGOs should be more 'accountable', but what they really seem to mean is that the NGO should act with more thoughtfulness, honesty, fidelity and probity. Recall the Encyclical of Pope Leo XIII in which he explained that associations need to be 'well and wisely administered'. The Pope also recognized that such ideal behaviour could not be forced by the 'grasp of a hand from without'. That insight remains relevant in our own time as we consider how to achieve better NGO performance in global governance. The grasp of a hand from without should be avoided in favour of a steadier hand from within and the invisible hand of the market.

Let me suggest the following framework to enhance NGO performance, specifically with reference to international advocacy activities. Rather than try to control what NGOs say and do, we should be improving the quality of public discourse so that good ideas from NGOs are more likely to be accepted by elected officials and bad ideas are more likely to be ignored. The way to improve the marketplace of ideas is to make it as competitive as possible among bureaucrats, NGOs and business participants. When NGO outputs are poor, they are not wholly to blame because they receive so little advice on how to be constructive. We live in an age of international standards and NGOs could certainly benefit from more refined standards as to what constitutes good practice in NGO advocacy. Some positive attributes are a high degree of transparency of NGO activities, an orientation toward data-driven analysis and strong internal governance mechanisms when an NGO operates in corporate form. In addition, governments owe it to the public and to the NGOs to enforce laws against NGOs that engage in illegal behaviour. Poor enforcement undermines the reputation of NGOs. In suggesting more attention be given to NGO performance, rather than to accountability, but in the words of Michael Edwards and David Hulme, 'assessing NGO performance is a difficult and messy business'.

Debunking NGO 'Representation'

Although the real issue in NGO accountability is whether the NGO is thoughtful, accurate and fair in its statements, most of the attention to NGO accountability has been on a different issue-that is, whether the NGO is representative of its members. To me, representation is simply a red herring. If the ideas being propounded are completely wrong, then the NGO for that reason may lack accountability to the community. In other words. If the adequacy of NGO representation of membership was ever a useful indicator of NGO accountability, surely the age of the internet and blogs changes that. For any powerful idea, a coordinator can put together many people in many countries who will support it. Such a virtual NGO might not have any organization in the traditional sense, but would be fully justified in saying that it faithfully represented its uniformly-thinking members. But surely the repetition or amplification of mistaken views is hardly sufficient for NGO accountability. Although much NGO activity occurs in traditional affinity organizations, we often see a phenomenon whereby the potential impact of governmental decisions creates a new constituency concerned about it (King, 2003). Individuals who may have little in common with each other will join an organization to promote a particular cause that unites them. Such temporary, single-issue organizations may be highly representative of membership, but their accountability should be judged more substantively.

Another representational critique of NGOs seems to be that NGOs are pursuing merely a partial interest, special interest or single issue, and so perforce NGOs will not be accountable to the public as a whole, which is motivated by general interests. Yet as philosophers have noted for centuries, ascertaining the general interest is no easy task. The US Supreme Court has declared that 'The two houses of Congress are legislative bodies representing larger constituencies'. Such representativeness is a source of the Congress's legitimacy, but the fact that there are two different houses suggests that neither was expected to be a perfect representative of the public. Acting in concert, however, they attempt to do so. Although NGOs may be a fixture of democracy, they are not themselves democratic institutions intended to represent the public in making decisions about the use of government power. NGOs do not compete with legislatures to represent public opinion.

At most, an NGO can represent a particular constituency or point of view. Yet the quality of its representation does not itself justify the NGO's role in influencing governmental outcomes. The representation of the public through elections is different from the nature of representing shared ideas and interests through an NGO. The root term 'represent' may get double duty, but representing ideas is different from representing voters. Kenneth Anderson (2000; 2001) is right that some NGOs have made exaggerated claims that they represent civil society or the public and right again that NGOs sometimes assert that their participation in global governance makes it more accountable.

The value derived from NGOs is not that they are better representatives of public opinion than are elected officials, or that NGOs supplement geographic representation via elections with interest group, pluralist representation. Those claims would not be justified and do not square with contemporary democratic theory. The true contribution of NGOs is that they seek to inform and influence the views of voters, elected officials and bureaucrats. That function of NGOs-to communicate information and values-fits comfortably in democratic theory because there is much more to democracy than the 'spasmodic majority vote'.

As Alexis de Tocqueville postulated in Democracy in America, 'no countries need associations more... than those with a democratic social state' (De Tocqueville, 1988). His monumental book explains a number of advantages for democracy of political and civic associations, including that associations contribute to 'stimulating competition', and that they allow members 'to discover the arguments most likely to make an impression on the majority'.

Thus, an NGO contributes to the democratic process by advocating its own view of the common good rather than by demonstrating that its view truly reflects the common will. The basics do not change when policy discourse crosses national borders (Marks, 2001). NGOs are not created by governments to operate solely within a domestic political space. NGOs emerge through 'spontaneous creation' and will want to pursue their agendas at whatever level of government they need to. John Bolton claims that 'it is precisely the detachment from governments that makes international civil society so troubling, at least for democracies' (Bolton, 2000).

Yet Bolton does not explain why he views voluntary associations as troubling when they detach themselves from government, other than to say that NGO participation in global governance 'provides a second opportunity for intrastate advocates to reargue their positions' and 'provides them at least the possibility of external lobbying leverage, to force domestic policy results they could not have otherwise achieved'.

There is no great need for special accountability for NGO advocacy functions in the public sphere. As voluntary organizations, NGOs depend on individuals who choose to belong to them, to work for them, to fund them and to listen to them. In 1999, the UN General Assembly endorsed strong freedom of association principles in the Declaration on the Right and Responsibility of Individuals, Groups and Organs of Society to Promote and Protect Universally Recognized Human Rights and Fundamental Freedoms. The Declaration states that 'Everyone has the right, individually and in association with others, to promote and to strive for the protection and realization of human rights and fundamental freedoms at the national and international levels' (UN, 1999, emphasis added). With respect to NGOs, the Declaration states, among other things, that 'Individuals, non-governmental organizations and relevant institutions have an important role to play in contributing to making the public more aware of questions relating to all human rights and fundamental freedoms'. This NGO role in making the public more aware is the key to understanding why NGO outputs injected into the marketplace of ideas are fully consistent with republican democracy.

Performance Versus Accountability in the Marketplace of Ideas

The best check on bad ideas from NGOs is criticism from others. Consider the recent episode of the spring 2005 report by Amnesty International that likened the US detention centres in Guantanamo to 'gulags'. President George Bush called that charge 'absurd' and Amnesty received considerable criticism for using a loaded term and making a claim for which they did not have evidence. This episode was valuable, however, in showing that a controversial statement by an NGO can be criticized by stakeholders and commentators, and that mistakes can hurt an NGO's reputation.

Such a market-like check is sufficient. The last thing the world needs is more governmental controls on Amnesty International to assure its accuracy and accountability. Common to the analyses by Edwards (2000) and Blitt (2004) is a conclusion that although NGOs could act voluntarily to develop standards to promote accountability, governments should not seek to impose such standards. NGOs tend to criticize governments, and so it will be difficult for governments to appear to be objective were they to police NGO statements as to whether they are honest and fair. The UN Panel of Eminent Persons that urges the UN Secretariat to engage NGOs in discussion about codes of conduct and self-policing mechanisms. In my view, that would be an inappropriate role for international bureaucrats.

The right way to promote better NGO behaviour is by fostering the continuation of present trends of increased introspection by NGOs about their own performance and new efforts by NGOs to evaluate one another. Instead of seeking to coerce NGOs into being more 'accountable', we should instead seek ways to enhance incentives for NGOs to upgrade their performance. Today, NGO performance is being monitored more than ever before-but in the right way, by other NGOs. For example, the American Enterprise Institute and the Federalist Society for Law and Public Policy Studies have jointly set up 'NGO Watch' in 'an effort to bring clarity and accountability to the burgeoning world of NGOs'. So far, their web site is largely composed of news stories, related documentation and policy papers, but perhaps some serious watching will occur.

Getting real mileage out of monitoring, or 'auditing' NGOs, as suggested by The Economist, requires the availability of performance standards that have been accepted by many NGOs. Standards would be very difficult to devise for advocacy, but could be doable for the operational activities of NGOs. In 2003, the Humanitarian Accountability Partnership International (HAP-I) was launched to improve the accountability of organizations engaged in delivering humanitarian services (Callamard in this volume). HAP-I promotes and assists self-monitoring by member organizations, which include well-known organizations such as CARE International and the Danish Refugee Council. The motto of HAP-I is 'making humanitarian action accountable to beneficiaries'. Another recent development is that Social Accountability International (SAI) has been asked by InterAction, an umbrella group of international charities, to inspect and certify the tsunami-related child sponsorship programs of five major NGOs (for example, Save the Children US). The certification requires allowing SAI to inspect documents and field activities, and also examines some management issues such as director conflicts of interest, accuracy of advertisements and a 35 per cent cap on administrative and fundraising costs relative to total expenditures.

New techniques are now being tested by governments to gain the benefits of NGO participation. One is multi-stakeholder roundtables or dialogues, which are sessions held during an intergovernmental summit or conference in which persons from governments, business and NGOs participate together in a discussion. Such dialogues were held, for example, at the UN Monterrey and Johannesburg Summits. Another technique is joint statements by a broad range of NGOs that are submitted to international conferences.

For example, in June 2004, at the United Nations Conference on Trade and Development XI, the Civil Society Forum submitted a Declaration that consisted of an analysis and several specific recommendations. The Declaration stated that the Forum 'represents social movements, pro-development groups, women's groups, trade unions, peasants and agricultural organizations, environmental organizations, faith-based organizations and fair trade organizations, among others'. This technique is distinguishable from the traditional parallel summit of NGOs that meets alongside an intergovernmental conference (Pianta, 2001).

The difference is that statements emanating from a parallel summit are not an official part of the intergovernmental meeting, as they were with the UNCTAD Forum. It may be too soon to tell whether these new forms of encouragement of NGOs to cooperate with each other will lead to more reasoned outputs. Yet such efforts are worth trying. After all, combining the value of autonomous groups with sustained cooperation among them is likely to contribute to economic and social progress. Democratic debate should not be subject to rigid zoning. Those who advocate ideas in one polity should be free to advocate them in another. When a transnational group gets together to promote a legitimate cause, it should be able to use its voice in any country or international organization. The idea that NGOs active in global governance lack sufficient accountability has become conventional wisdom. Because NGOs are extremely sensitive to threats to their influence, they can be expected to take steps to obviate those threats. Recognizing that NGO influence is now being undermined to some extent by the mantra for greater NGO accountability, NGOs will be eager to cooperate in the expansion of 'accountability' mechanisms.

An attempt to formulate a plan for greater government regulation of NGO political activities would run into many problems, starting with the trammels of statism. Government regulation tends to be territorial and yet this does not match up well with the domain of NGO action that can be global, or with the membership and participants in an NGO that can be transnational. The difficulty of this spatial challenge tends to be underestimated by those who would like to see greater NGO accountability to someone or something. It is one thing to say that Global Witness, for example, needs to be more accountable, but quite another to specify to what sovereign authority or global public accountability is to be owed.

Governments should not try to regulate directly the quality of advocacy of NGOs, but rather should improve it indirectly by establishing mechanisms that give NGOs an incentive to upgrade their own performance. NGOs are very likely to be criticizing governments and it will be difficult for governments to appear to be objective were they to supervise NGO statements. The idea of providing better mechanisms for NGO debate works well whether the issues are technical/scientific or hinge on values.

The WTO benefited enormously from the intellectual contributions of health NGOs who pointed out that the trade rule for compulsory licensing of patents could prevent a supply of essential medicines from being available to countries without a manufacturing capacity. That point was an economic and technical one. The NGO critics of WTO Agreement on Trade-Related Aspects of Intellectual Property Rights (TRIPS) also raised more general concerns about whether the WTO rules for patenting took sufficient account of health values.

Over many decades, NGOs have shown themselves to be adept in advocacy on both the narrower technical points and the broader claims on values. In the critiques of NGOs, one subtext seems to be that NGOs are pursuing only a 'partial' interest (or a single-issue campaign), and perforce NGOs will not be accountable to the public as a whole, which is motivated by general interests. Assuming that this is true and a problem, the solution might be to pay less attention to the NGOs or to mandate group altruism.

In my view, that is the wrong diagnosis and the wrong solution. It is the wrong diagnosis because partiality or private interest can operate as a virtue not only in markets but also in polities. Constitutional rules may be valuable to tie a government's hands in order to make it less susceptible to the entreaties of special interests, but in my view, such constitutional rules should not include muzzling the private voice. It is the wrong solution because authoritative decision-makers need a constant infusion of competitive ideas and values in order to make the right public policy decisions. To quote De Tocqueville (1988), 'A government, by itself, is equally incapable of refreshing the circulation of feelings and ideas among a great people, as it is of controlling every industrial undertaking'.

Government bureaucrats and politicians do not have any special competence to oversee NGO operations and guide them towards attainment of the common good. Ideally, any ensuing regulatory or accountability mechanisms should be devised by NGOs themselves as voluntary measures.

5

Civil Society Legitimacy and Accountability: Issues and Challenges

In the last twenty years, the roles of civil society organizations—community-based organizations, churches, development NGOs, relief agencies, advocacy coalitions—have grown explosively. While there are many differences across regions and countries, researchers still suggest that the trends amount to a "global associational revolution" that has major implications for governance and social problem-solving. A recent UN report suggests that "civil society is as much a part of today's global governance as governments," and many see central roles for civil society organizations (CSOs) in coping with the critical challenges that confront our increasingly interdependent world.

To fulfil this promise, however, CSOs must themselves grapple with clarifying their legitimacy as social and political actors and their accountabilities to key stakeholders that ensure that they contribute to the public good. Dealing with these issues will help CSOs define more clearly their missions and values and position them to learn more effectively from their experience. Better answers to questions about legitimacy and accountability can help mobilize staffs, allies, and public support. While CSOs have often been remarkably effective at holding governments and corporations accountable to policies and promises, their continued effectiveness will turn on their capacity to live up to their own standards. Therefore there are both internal and external reasons for attention to these issues.

This paper teases apart some of the complexities of civil society legitimacy and accountability and describes examples of the growing array of systems and practices for responding to legitimacy and accountability challenges. It offers a framework for understanding the concepts of legitimacy and accountability, and then suggests approaches to enhancing the legitimacy and accountability of civil society organizations and multi-organization domains. While it provides examples of efforts to grapple with these issues, the paper is not intended to provide detailed "how-to" advice for dealing with specific legitimacy and accountability challenges. Such advice is available, however, at many of the websites and organizations described in the paper.

The next section looks at issues of civil society legitimacy and accountability and suggests why they have become so important. The third section provides a framework for understanding these issues and ways to address them. It describes our definitions of legitimacy and accountability, their interaction in the context of civil society missions and strategies, and several sources of standards of legitimacy and accountability. The fourth section describes ways to build organizational accountability systems that can enhance the legitimacy and accountability of civil society actors. Such systems can be used to catalyze organizational learning and capacity building as well as to increase accountability and legitimacy. The fifth section focuses on building the legitimacy and accountability of multi-organization domains. Such domains include campaign alliances, sectors of similar organizations, and problem domains that involve diverse actors. The sixth section briefly discusses the evolution of societal standards of legitimacy and accountability. The seventh section describes some ongoing dilemmas that we expect will challenge and energize future debates. The last section provides a brief conclusion.

Overall, this report aims to contribute to local, national and global discourses and debates about civil society legitimacy and accountability. We also hope it will help catalyze action at many levels to resolve questions posed by these debates.

Why Legitimacy and Accountability?

Why are legitimacy and accountability issues problematic for civil society organizations? In part the issues are inherent in the nature of civil society and in part they are a result of special circumstances that have emerged in the last twenty-five years.

The nature of civil society as a sector contributes to questions about legitimacy and accountability in several ways. For example, CSOs often mobilize people and resources through commitments to social values and missions that enhance the public good. Their reputation as legitimate and accountable stewards of those missions is vital to their ability to recruit staff and allies to their causes. Gandhi and the Indian Independence Movement, Martin Luther King Jr. and the Civil Rights Movement, and Solidarity and the Polish Liberation Movement all depended on their legitimacy as embodiments of widely held social values to mobilize support and credibility. If CSOs leave questions about their legitimacy and accountability unanswered, they risk undermining organizational identities and capacities that depend on values and voluntary commitments.

A second common attribute of CSOs is that they have diverse stakeholders that make competing accountability claims. Unlike a corporation that is ultimately accountable to owners and shareholders or a democratic government that is accountable to voters, CSOs are not primarily accountable to any clearly defined stakeholders. Civil society organizations, in contrast, are accountable to many stakeholders: to donors for their resources, to clients for delivery of goods and services, to allies for performance of joint activities, to staff and members for meeting their expectations, and to government agencies for complying with regulations. They are also accountable to their missions. Dealing with diverse accountability claims may be extremely difficult, and where stakeholders have different or contradictory interests, being fully accountable to all of them is impossible. So accountability is a challenging problem for CSOs because of the nature of the sector and its relations to stakeholders.

A third attribute of many CSOs is their predilection for taking up issues on behalf of poor and marginalized groups. While this bias can be the basis for raising funds and support from charitable donations, it may also require challenging powerful constituencies whose interests may be harmed by proposed changes. Those constituencies may see such challenges as irresponsible or unwise at best: Gandhi, King and Solidarity all took on powerful actors who regarded their initiatives as illegitimate if not outright subversive. Issues of civil society legitimacy and accountability have emerged as particularly important in the last five years due to several factors. First, many questions about civil society reflect concerns about the legitimacy and accountability of many institutions. Concerns about corruption in government agencies and unacceptable practices by business organizations are often as urgent as concerns about civil society. Illegal activities at Enron in the US or Bofors in India raise questions about both business and government accountability. The impacts of such events can spread throughout societies, affecting public perceptions of many institutions. In part the growing concern about legitimacy and accountability reflects a general "crisis of governance."

Second, some legitimacy and accountability questions grow out of problematic behaviour on the part of some civil society organizations. Publicity about the accusations of board self-dealing at The Nature Conservancy or the mistaken analysis made by Greenpeace of the proposed Brent Spar oilrig disposal in the North Sea raise questions about whether CSOs live up to their professed values and whether mechanisms exist to enforce minimum standards of practice. CSOs, like many other organizations, are not uniformly altruistic nor are their actions always consistent with their values. Some challenges to their legitimacy grow out of their own mistakes or malfeasance.

Third, some current challenges to CSO legitimacy and accountability come from agencies that have been targets of civil society advocacy activities. When CSOs exert political and social pressure on behalf of marginalized constituencies, for example, they may inspire counterattacks by powerful interests. Government agencies charged with corruption, corporations pressed to change bad business practices, and intergovernmental institutions challenged to alter projects or policies have often questioned the legitimacy and the accountability of their challengers.8 Of course, it is important that CSOs explain their legitimacy and their accountability to key stakeholders, but sometimes those criticisms are inspired by motives other than an altruistic desire for transparency.

All these demands on CSOs have been further complicated by their expanding roles in the sphere of social development and change. Civil society actors in the past have often been seen as "gap fillers," providing services not available from the market or the state. However, in recent years they have increasingly taken on capacity building and policy advocacy roles that make them participants in multi-sectoral governance processes. While much civil society work has historically been focused on local problems, CSOs now increasingly work at national and transnational levels as well. Their emerging roles in large-scale initiatives require new attention to the issues of legitimacy and accountability.

CIVIL SOCIETY LEGITIMACY AND ACCOUNTABILITY: A FRAMEWORK

We focus here on the concepts of legitimacy and accountability and their implications for enhancing the legitimacy and accountability of civil society actors. Then we will explore

the interactions between legitimacy and accountability. Legitimacy and accountability are concepts that can be applied at many levels: individuals, groups, organizations, interorganizational domains, societies, and so on. Our focus here is on legitimacy and accountability for organizations and domains—the arenas most immediately available for influence by civil society actors themselves.

Legitimacy

The concept of legitimacy refers to perceptions by key stakeholders that the existence, activities and impacts of CSOs are justifiable and appropriate in terms of central social values and institutions. For example, Edwards has defined legitimacy as "the right to be and do something in society—a sense that an organization is lawful, admissible, and justified in its chosen course of action." Legitimacy is grounded in the perceptions of stakeholders in the larger environment in which the organization is embedded. The concept has been most developed in thinking about political systems, but it has also been a matter of recent concern for development institutions and civil society actors. At least four kinds of legitimacy are important for CSOs. These forms of legitimacy are largely the product of external forces and dynamics that are not under the direct control of CSOs. They include:

- Legal Legitimacy: Legitimacy can grow from compliance with legal and regulatory requirements, such as meeting state registration requirements or following national laws and codes that define appropriate CSO activity. CSOs that have been certified by the Philippine Council for NGO Certification, for example, have gained legal status that enables their donors to deduct contributions from their taxes. This form of legitimacy draws on the authorizing power of the state and its legislation.

- Normative Legitimacy: Claims to CSO legitimacy can also be grounded in widely held social values, norms and standards. CSOs with normative legitimacy are assessed as meeting norms for performance ("it does good work"), as implementing desired structures and processes ("it represents its constituents"), for fitting the task ("CSOs are good for grassroots organizing"), or for the characteristics of its leaders and staff ("its leaders are committed and effective"). Normative legitimacy is particularly important for CSOs since they are often value-based organizations that emphasize contributions to the public good at the heart of their missions.

- Pragmatic Legitimacy: The legitimacy of CSOs may also emerge from the instrumental value they provide to various stakeholders, either directly in terms of specific outputs or more generally in terms of creating conditions that meet stakeholder interests. Service or advocacy organizations may provide immediate benefits to stakeholders and so be perceived as legitimate; they may also contribute to creating more general contexts (better public health; more responsive government agencies) that are favourable to stakeholders and so gain their support.
- Cognitive Legitimacy. CSOs are also perceived as legitimate when their activities and goals are widely seen as appropriate, proper, and "making sense" to the larger society. Cognitive legitimacy may emerge from acceptance of organizational activities as fitting into a comprehensible and acceptable story about their roles in society. It may also emerge from widespread perceptions that the organization is a social institution that is "taken for granted" by the society as being part of "the way things are." This is true, for example, for churches and some educational institutions in many societies.

Institutional legitimacy is derived from the perceptions

of external observers and stakeholders. These perceptions are often the product of complex interactions and forces that are beyond the control of CSOs. But we can identify at least four approaches that offer CSOs opportunities to enhance their legitimacy. The first three focus on aligning the CSO with existing legitimacy contexts and the CSO; the last emphasizes creating new stories and definitions of legitimacy when existing contexts are changing or responding to innovation.

- Conform to existing models of legitimate organizations. CSOs can adopt structures, procedures and systems that make the agency resemble other organizations that are widely perceived as legitimate. Adopting governance arrangements used by other agencies in the field, for example, can confer legitimacy. This approach draws on existing legal, normative and cognitive bases of legitimacy to enhance external perceptions of the organization.
- Inform external stakeholders in legitimated terms. CSOs can describe their activities in terms that draw on existing legitimacy standards and expectations. This approach may utilize pragmatic legitimacy by emphasizing the agency's contributions to particular stakeholders, or it may frame the CSO's story to emphasize widely held legal, normative or cognitive expectations.
- Manipulate myths, symbols and ceremonies to build cognitive legitimacy. CSOs can use existing cognitive expectations to shape stakeholder perceptions of their legitimacy. Adopting monitoring and evaluation schemes approved by donors, for example, may enhance CSO legitimacy

with those donors even if the CSO does not use them for active learning or capacity building.

- Construct new definitions and standards of legitimacy. Aligning CSO activities with existing standards can support the very status quo the CSO seeks to change. It may be necessary to challenge existing laws, norms, cognitions, and interests to construct legitimacy consistent with a desired social transformation. CSOs can reframe existing definitions to demonstrate their negative consequences and use their experience to articulate new understanding of legitimate goals. The women's movement, for example, redefined the nature of "human rights" to include private violence against women as well as state abuses, a reframing that implies a positive state duty to intervene to protect women even in the private spaces of their households.

These strategies move from pure alignment with existing expectations to actively changing the expectations that underpin legitimacy judgments. While aligning the CSO with existing standards of legitimacy is easier than constructing new standards, for some CSOs creating new standards lies at the heart of their development task. We will return to the issues of constructing new standards later in this report.

Accountability

The concept of accountability has been defined in many ways, not all of them compatible or mutually reinforcing. We will focus on accountability as a responsibility to answer for particular performance expectations to specific stakeholders. So, unlike the general contextual expectations that shape the legitimacy of CSOs, accountability may focus on quite specific claims—from financial accounting practices, to quality of services delivered, to advocacy campaign tactics utilized. CSO values, missions and strategies define goals and activities for which they might be held accountable by these stakeholders.

For CSOs it is often difficult to identify stakeholders who have primacy in their accountability claims. In other sectors primary stakeholders are often well-established: private sector firms owe primary accountability to owners and stockholders, and public agencies in democracies are accountable to voters and their elected representatives. CSOs, in contrast, are often accountable to many stakeholders, and therefore not primarily accountable to any. CSOs may owe accountability upward to donors who provide resources and to regulators responsible for their legal certification, downward to beneficiaries and clients who use their services or to members who expect representation, outward to allies and peers who cooperate in programs and projects, and inward to staff and volunteers who invest their talents and time in organizational activities.

But it is not obvious which of these claimants has priority when their demands are not compatible. Without accountability to donors, funding sources may dry up; without accountability to regulators, charters may be revoked; without accountability to beneficiaries, services may not be used; without accountability to staff and volunteers, operational capacity may be eroded; without accountability to members and political constituents, credibility may be undermined. It is common for conflicts among accountability claims to be resolved in favour of stakeholders with the power to punish the CSO for lack of attention: Donors and regulators, for example, often get more accountability attention than beneficiaries or staff. But that resolution of conflicting claims does not always advance CSO missions, particularly when they seek to foster self-reliance, improved services, capacity-building, or political voice for marginalized populations. How tradeoffs are made among stakeholders with conflicting claims is a critical issue to which we will return later.

It is also critical to understand the nature of accountability relationships. Several quite different models of accountability relations have emerged from work in different sectors.

- In government circles, for example, a commonly used model is representative accountability, which emphasizes the obligations of representatives to their constituents. This model has roots in political theory and is often applied to public sector actors expected to be democratically accountable to voters or their elected representatives. It is particularly relevant to CSOs that represent members or constituents to give political voice to otherwise unheard interests. The civil society campaign against the Narmada dams in India, for example, claimed to represent thousands of small farmers who would be displaced, and drew much of its legitimacy with stakeholders like the World Bank from its ability to speak credibly for those grassroots constituents. In representative accountability, violations of constituent mandates can lead to replacement of elected leadership.
- In the business world the most widely used model is principal-agent accountability, which focuses on motivating agents to achieve the goals of their

principals. From this perspective, the major challenge is to design incentives that will keep the agent faithful to the principal's interests. Principal-agent accountability emphasizes the fiduciary responsibilities of agents and economic and legal incentives to encourage agents to act for principals. Violations of contract accountabilities can be enforced through the legal system with financial or legal sanctions. Donors often fund CSOs as agents to carry out tasks that the donors cannot accomplish by themselves, and donors often set standards of financial and program accountability to be met by their agents.

- A third model that is particularly relevant to CSOs focuses on creating mutual accountability compacts that bind members through shared values, aspirations and social identities. The parties to mutual accountability define shared goals and "buy in" to responsibility for achieving them. Sanctions for violating expectations are social and relational, so relationships and trust become critical elements in the construction and implementation of shared analyses and plans. Mutually accountable relationships require developing shared understanding, respect, trust, and mutual influence. They may require more time and energy to create and they are more difficult to maintain across large numbers of actors than agency contracts or representative mandates. But many CSOs that build alliances across levels and regions to gain leverage find mutual accountability appropriate for dealing with the uncertainties they face.

CSOs use different models of accountability with

different stakeholders. Relations with donors often depend on principal-agent negotiations and contracts; relations with members may be organized around representative accountability of elected leaders; and relations with allies may depend on mutual accountability grounded in histories of mutual trust and cooperation. Relations constructed as one model may evolve over time into another, as when a long-term relationship between a donor and a CSO evolves from a principal-agent contract for specific outcomes to a more mutually accountable compact to accomplish shared social objectives. When parties understand their relationship in terms of different underlying models, serious problems can arise. Many Northern and Southern CSOs, for example, use the language of mutual accountability in constructing "partnerships," and when Northern CSOs—sometimes under pressure from their own donors—invoke principal-agent concepts to administer the partnership, their Southern colleagues feel misled or betrayed.

Since accountability relations involve specific relationships and expectations, they are more subject to direct influence by CSOs than legitimacy perceptions. After an elaborate analysis of accountabilities for intergovernmental organizations, multinational corporations, and transnational civil society associations, the Global Accountabilities

Project identified four core accountability mechanisms that are critical to managing accountability claims. These mechanisms are starting points for accountability management strategies with both internal and external stakeholders.

Transparency mechanisms enable the free flow of information between organizations and stakeholders in decision making, performance and reporting. Reporting and disclosure systems and processes that enable information sharing among parties are central to an effective accountability relationship. Examples include audited accounts and annual reports made available to stakeholders. Participation mechanisms enable internal and external stakeholders to be involved in organizational decision making. Key stakeholder involvement in deciding about goals and activities may be critical to eventual accountability for their performance. Participation mechanisms include regular consultations with stakeholders or inclusion of stakeholder representatives on Boards of Directors.

Evaluation mechanisms make it possible for stakeholders as well as the CSO to assess activities, outputs, outcomes and impacts. Monitoring and assessing results enables judgments about the success of organizational efforts in meeting its performance premises. Examples include organizational monitoring and evaluation systems, independent program evaluations, and social audits.

Complaints and redress mechanisms provide vehicles for raising questions about CSO performance and for sanctioning failures to deliver on performance goals.

These mechanisms are particularly important when large inequalities in power between the CSO and key stakeholders might undermine the capacities of stakeholders to demand accountability. Review panels, juries and ombudsmen are examples of ways to create opportunities for complaints and redress by many stakeholders.

Efforts to manage accountabilities to CSO stakeholders can focus on one or several of these mechanisms. The forms the mechanisms take vary across accountability models, since the underlying relationship characteristics are quite different. The models of accountability relationships and their differing requirements for core accountability mechanisms. For representative accountability, for example, voters need mechanisms that enable transparency and evaluation of representative performance, such as publication of votes or a free press that investigates and publicizes representative activities. Voter participation in setting priorities and shaping decisions require regular interaction with representatives. Complaints and redress issues can be raised by media or oversight agencies that influence voter actions in elections.

For principal-agent accountability, principals must negotiate contracts that specify performance expectations, reporting arrangements, and rewards and punishments for various outcomes. Contract provisions can be written to build transparency on critical issues and systems for evaluating performance, and the parties can rely on third parties, such as courts, to help enforce those contracts.

For mutual accountability, the parties must develop shared goals and perspectives and relationships of mutual respect and trust that can underpin their compact. Such compacts depend on two-way sharing of information and participation in key decisions and on evaluation systems focused on agreed responsibilities for achieving shared goals. Complaints and redress turn on peer relations and participants' commitment to maintaining their social identities and reputations.

Legitimacy, Accountability and Sources of Standards

Legitimacy and accountability influence each other. CSO legitimacy reflects generalized perceptions of the organization by actors in its environment. Those perceptions may be influenced by management strategies that align organizational goals and activities to fit environmental expectations or (with more difficulty) reconstruct environmental expectations to fit the organization. Accountabilities describe more focused expectations that are held by specific CSO stakeholders. Improving accountability to appropriate stakeholders can strengthen CSO legitimacy by clarifying the interests they serve and how abuses can be controlled. Questions about the legitimacy of CSOs are often raised in accountability terms: "Who elected them?" "Who holds them accountable?"

Defining the accountabilities of CSOs and how they are enforced is probably the single most powerful intervention for preserving and enhancing their legitimacy as social actors. But how are such standards and enforcement processes defined? And to what extent can CSOs influence the substance of accountability standards and the processes by which they will be enforced? We believe that there are three sources of accountability standards that are important for civil society: (1) established societal ideals reflected in laws or widely held norms and expectations; (2) negotiated domain standards created by communities of organizations to govern a common area of work; and (3) strategic organizational choices about standards and stakeholders that govern the activities of particular CSOs.

Established societal ideals are standards for accountability rooted in legal traditions, social norms or cognitive expectations. CSOs are expected to obey basic laws and norms of their societies, and governments may create specific regulations for their formation, resources, and activities. Social norms and "customs having the force of law" also create societal ideals. When very high salaries for chief executives of some charitable organizations in the US became public knowledge, many donors reduced their contributions because the organizations had violated widely-held norms about reasonable compensation in the nonprofit sector. Some national governments have sought more rigorous state regulation of civil society organizations in response to perceived abuses, though such regulation may also create significant costs in undermining the sector flexibility and ease of entry that generates social energy and innovation.

Sometimes civil society and government agencies cooperate to jointly develop societal standards. The evolution of the Philippines Council for NGO Certification (PCNC) as an effort to negotiate and enforce standards for the NGO sector in cooperation with government agencies, so that the resulting standards are responsive to the concerns of both sectors.

The PCNC experience demonstrates that codes of conduct and peer reviews can control the proliferation of fraudulent NGOs and build a shared base for recognizing good practice, though the certification process has also required substantial commitments of volunteer time and energy. Such initiatives can catalyze cross-sector and society-wide debate on the elements of a code of conduct and help construct understanding and commitment to minimum standards. State support in the form of tax relief invests the PCNC standards with the status of societal ideals.

A second source of standards is the creation of negotiated domain standards that take into account the specialized experience and expertise of communities of organizations. Such domain standards can be negotiated to set accountability expectations in multi-organizational contexts that range from communities of organizations in the same sector, to campaign coalitions across local, national, and regional differences, to intersectoral partnerships that bring together business, government, civil society and other actors to solve shared problems.

Initiatives to build domain standards out of organizational experience and to certify compliance with those standards is becoming increasingly common for NGOs in many countries, from Pakistan and India to Australia and the United States. The Code of Conduct for NGOs in Ethiopia, which grew out of discussions among many NGOs concerned about fostering greater accountability in the sector. The Code Observance section provides for the Code Observance Committee to hear complaints and decide about code violations, including membership suspension or cancellation if necessary.

Creating sector standards can provide opportunities for constructive debate about CSO practices and problems as well as avenues to greater financial support from many sources. But building detailed standards is not easy. It is often relatively easy to come to agreement on general principles, but creating detailed standards and mechanisms for sanctioning violations of those standards may be very difficult. The NGO Code for Ethiopia, for example, created a Committee of NGO leaders and civil society leaders to hear complaints and take action on Code violations.

A third source of accountability standards is organizational strategic choice. Organizations may have considerable leeway in defining how much they will emphasize accountability to various stakeholders, particularly when their stakeholders vary in interests and power. Those choices have consequences, of course. CSOs cannot choose to ignore stakeholders without legal, moral or prudential risks. But CSOs often make less use of space for choice than they could. In the absence of strategic thinking about the issues of accountability, some stakeholders receive much more attention than others. It is common for donors and government regulators to have their accountability claims honoured, while the claims of less powerful constituencies like poor and marginalized beneficiaries receive less attention. While CSOs often complain about having to comply with donor-or government-imposed accountability standards, they often give little attention to the possibilities of balancing those demands with increased attention to other stakeholders' claims.

But such imbalances are not automatic. Organizations can make strategic choices about accountabilities to different stakeholders and even create systems that enhance the abilities of low-power stakeholders to influence performance. The strategic choices of PRIA in India to manage conflicting accountabilities to stakeholders in civil society capacity-building initiatives. Accountability standards can be articulated at the organizational, domain, and societal levels. Where there is widespread agreement on the kinds of goals and activities that are most appropriate, legislation or "customs having the force of law" can codify expectations into societal ideals. Where the issues are less well-understood or more controversial, societal agreement on which to ground legislated regulations or normative standards may not yet exist. When innovative responses to poorly understood problems are needed to build the base for societal ideals, domain negotiations to set standards based on experience across organizations or organizational strategic choices by those grappling with the problems may be more appropriate sources of standards. The experience of such organizations may provide the base for domain negotiations, and the articulation of domain standards may be precursors to societal ideals. In the sections that follow, we focus on building accountability systems for organizations and domains because they offer CSOs opportunities to actively influence their own accountability and legitimacy.

CONSTRUCTING ORGANIZATIONAL ACCOUNTABILITY SYSTEMS

The missions and strategies of civil society organizations are at the heart of defining their legitimacy and accountability. Criteria for legitimacy and accountability vary across missions and strategies. Service delivery CSOs may be required to demonstrate the quality and reach of their services and make themselves accountable to donors and service regulators to get critical resources. Capacity building CSOs may work closely with clients to develop programs and so emphasize accountability to clients whose active cooperation is essential to co-producing enhanced capacities. Advocacy CSOs may need to build legitimacy with both the constituents they represent and the targets they seek to influence. Accountability to constituents is central to preserving their legitimacy as a voice for otherwise unheard populations; legitimacy with targets is necessary to effectively influencing them. In the multi-stakeholder world of CSOs different missions may demand different priorities among stakeholder accountabilities.

CSOs that do not grapple with the issues of legitimacy and accountability often pay more attention to stakeholders with loud voices and substantial power—such as donors and government agencies—and pay less attention to stakeholders with less clout—such as clients or agency staff. In this section we turn explicitly to the possibilities of building systems for managing accountabilities to many stakeholders. Such accountability systems include definitions of performance, identification of key stakeholders, tools for assessing performance, mechanisms for communicating those assessments, and vehicles for creating performance consequences for the CSO.

The links among CSO strategies, activities and results. The "strategic triangle" of value creation, legitimacy and support, and operational capacity on the left, reflects three critical questions that CSO leaders must answer in creating organizational strategy. It is important for CSO leaders to define (1) what and how it will create value (such as services delivered, capacities built, or policies influenced), (2) how it can gain support and legitimacy for its work, and (3) how it will develop the operational capability to carry out its strategy.

The CSO carries out activities to create value (such as health services, capacity-building workshops, or policy analyses) which in turn contribute to outcomes such as changed behaviour by targets (such as better nutrition by mothers, more self-help by villagers, changed policies by legislators) which foster longer-term social impacts (such as healthier babies, improved village conditions, and improved government services). These elements together comprise the CSO's value chain or change theory for accomplishing its strategy and mission.

Accountability systems assess information about activities, outputs, outcomes and impacts, report results to relevant stakeholders, and enable stakeholders to hold the CSO accountable. Thus the dashed arrows from the accountability system reflect the use of performance information to enhance legitimacy and support, strengthen organizational capacity, and enhance value creation.

Articulating Strategies and Value Chains

Clarifying CSO strategies for accomplishing their missions is a critical step in building accountability systems that support mission accomplishment. Different strategies utilize different chains of activities, outputs and outcomes to produce desired long-term impacts. Service delivery (such as providing micro-credit loans), capacity building (such as training entrepreneurs), and policy advocacy (such as promoting small business-friendly legislation) are strategies that imply quite different activities and desired results, though all three might be used to enhance the incomes of impoverished populations. The value to be created is linked to approaches to generating legitimacy and support and constructing operational capability. So, articulating the CSO's fundamental strategy is an important step in building an accountability system.

Strategies usually include a theory about how the CSO's activities will produce long-term impacts. Such theories have been discussed as "change theories" or "logic models" or "value chains." 25 In essence they describe how the CSO believes its work will make a difference. CSOs have considerable control over the nature of their immediate outputs, such as loans provided or workshops delivered. They have less control over how those outputs are utilized by their clients or targets, and still less influence over how the behaviour of clients and targets interacts with other factors over the longer term to produce social impacts. PRIA's value chain for CSO organization development, for example, assumed that effective organization development depended on creating client relationships that enabled frank discussion of organizational problems. Their theory implies that client mistrust would undermine the outcomes necessary to achieve desired impacts. Articulating strategies and their value chains is central to understanding points at which accountability to various stakeholders is critical to mission accomplishment.

Identifying and Prioritizing Organizational Stakeholders

Who are the key stakeholders for CSOs? Answers to this question vary considerably across CSOs, depending on their missions and strategies, the contextual forces they face, and the capacities they bring to bear. The stakeholders that are critical to disaster relief or service provision may be quite different from those central to local capacity building or to policy advocacy. Since CSOs have many diverse stakeholders—donors, members, regulators, clients, allies, staffs, targets—trying to be fully accountable to all of them may be a recipe for paralysis or constant firefighting. Prioritizing accountabilities can be vital to mission accomplishment.

The strategic triangle offers a simple way to identify and map stakeholders who have important accountability claims by focusing on value creation, legitimacy and support, and operational capability. The strategic triangle to identify stakeholders of an international NGO that builds the capacities of marginalized communities, Southern NGOs, and local government agencies.

When the relevant stakeholders have been identified, CSO leaders can assess the nature and importance of accountabilities on at least three dimensions. First, is the CSO accountable on legal grounds? Some stakeholders can use law and the courts to hold the CSO accountable, such as suing it to compel compliance with contractual obligations to provide donors with audited accounts. Second, is the CSO accountable on normative grounds? Some stakeholders can call for accountability on grounds of values and norms held by the CSO, such as publicizing CSO behaviour that is inconsistent with its public value and norm commitments. And third, is the CSO accountable on prudential or practical grounds? Some stakeholders can exact high costs for accountability failures, as in donors refusing to re-fund programs.

Stakeholders may have claims on several grounds. Donors often have strong claims on legal and prudential grounds, while clients may have strong moral claims but little prudential clout or legal standing. One approach has been to assess stakeholders on all three questions and then combine those assessments for an overall priority rating. Identifying stakeholders and establishing priorities among them is essential to constructing accountability systems that support mission and strategy achievement. Many CSOs recognize the temptation to pay more attention to stakeholders with strong prudential and legal claims and pay less attention to value-based claims, even when those values are at the core of CSO missions. Recognizing and discussing those tensions is central to constructing accountability systems that realistically support CSO missions.

Setting Standards and Measuring Performance

Accountability systems depend on agreements about performance and how it can be measured. Measuring performance is particularly challenging when CSOs seek to accomplish long-term social impacts, since it is difficult to measure precisely such impacts or the contributions of various actors to them. Articulating value chains provides a framework to evaluate indicators for assessing immediate outputs, client outcomes, and longer-term impacts—but the causes of those indicators are increasingly difficult to assess as they become more distant from CSO activities.

The challenges of assessing social and environmental impacts have received increasing attention in the last ten years. While many initiatives have examined ways to assess immediate outputs of programs, others have paid attention to their outcomes in terms of changed behaviour on the part of program targets. The work of organizations like the New Economics Foundation, Accountability, and Keystone, for example, have contributed to expanding awareness of measures and standards for assessing social and environmental impacts. With cooperation from a number of universities, the practitioner-led Social Performance Management system (SPM) supports microfinance institutions to measure social as well as financial performance and to build new forms of accountability.

It is not uncommon for donors to require evaluation plans for the programs they fund. But donor interests differ from interests of other stakeholders, and their evaluations may not serve other stakeholders well. Indeed, some CSOs collect information required by donors but create quite different systems to support their own learning. The challenges of creating performance measurement systems that serve multiple stakeholders have inspired a number of innovations, such as the OSANGO assessment system. Note that this approach emphasizes working with stakeholders— particularly clients and beneficiaries—to define problems, identify indicators and measures of impact, and assess and interpret results. The system is designed to foster joint learning about program outcomes and impacts, stressing enhanced independence and capacity of program clients as well as learning for the CSO.

ASSESSING AND COMMUNICATING PERFORMANCE

The results of CSO performance can be assessed in many ways. The data from performance indicators developed in the prior step must be analysed, interpreted and communicated to key stakeholders if they are to hold the organization accountable. Some organizations invest time and resources in self-evaluations, deploying staff to collect and analyse information about program performance and how much their activities have the impacts intended. Others commission external evaluations (or have evaluations imposed on them) to gain the advantage of technically sophisticated and organizationally independent feedback.

Communications include disclosure statements, annual reports, or publication of internal and external evaluations. Writing reports in English may be useful for donors, but it does not help clients who are not literate English-speakers understand what the CSO is doing. The critical issue here is making information available in forms that are comprehensible and useful to various stakeholders. Stakeholder diversity means, of course, that some will find communications more difficult to decipher than others.

An important initiative in assessing and reporting CSO impacts has been the rise of social auditing. Much of the initial work in this area has focused on private sector initiatives, but it is highly relevant to CSO work as well. Social auditing develops indicators and tools for assessing social and environmental impacts as well as economic results. A particularly interesting innovation in the area of assessing and communicating performance is the Keystone initiative. This initiative builds on the assumption that better performance and reporting standards will expand the resources available for social programs.

CREATING PERFORMANCE CONSEQUENCES

Since the interests and capacities of CSO stakeholders vary, making information available to all of them in the same format does not ensure that they can hold the CSO accountable. While government officials and donor agency staff may be quite happy with audited accounts or external evaluation reports, grassroots constituents may not have the languages (e.g., English) or the skills (e.g., accounting) to interpret the reports. Even if they understand the reports they may not have the power or the resources to compel attention to their concerns. "Creating performance consequences" assumes some degree of voice and influence from the relevant stakeholders and some power to ensure that CSOs have strong incentives to listen to relevant stakeholders.

This problem is often recognized by CSOs—but less often solved. An initiative by an international NGO concerned with the difficulties of managing information from local assessments while promoting enhanced local accountability. 4.6 Organizational Learning, Operational Capacity and Legitimacy

The information generated by accountability systems

has a number of uses. It offers opportunities to organizations operating in complex and changing contexts for organizational learning from information about program outputs, outcomes and impacts.

This information can help the CSO learn what works at the operational level as well as how accurately its theories of change in fact predict and explain results. The dashed arrow from the accountability system to the creating value aspect of the CSO strategy reflects the organization's ability to adapt by making use of organizational learning.

Within the organization, information from the accountability system can be used for operational capacity-building, clarifying roles and responsibilities and defining performance expectations to focus organizational energies where they will have the greatest impact. The accountability system to operational capability indicates the possibility of using new information to foster more effective performance.

Finally, the existence of clear standards and information about performance can be used to strengthen internal and external legitimacy of the CSO, as indicated by the dashed arrow from the accountability system to legitimacy and support.

The more clearly the organization can produce data that indicates mission-related performance and impacts, the more credible the case for legitimacy. Critics may challenge the relevance or value of the mission–but at a minimum the CSO can demonstrate that its actions are consistent with its words–that it "walks its own talk" in behaving consistently with its values.

In short, constructing accountability systems at the organizational level offers CSO leaders opportunities to assess the importance of various stakeholders and design systems that align internal and external accountabilities to press for mission accomplishment. Defining organizational accountabilities makes it possible for key stakeholders to support accomplishment of critical objectives.

There is no complete freedom to decide which accountabilities will be primary—accountability choices have consequences, particularly when powerful stakeholders get less than they want. But donors and regulators may recognize the importance of accountability to other stakeholders—particularly those whose capacity and empowerment is the rationale for the programs they support. There is enough latitude for many CSO leaders, given chances to negotiate with donors and other stakeholders, to build accountability systems that support and reinforce their strategic commitments.

BUILDING DOMAIN ACCOUNTABILITY SYSTEMS

Civil society legitimacy and accountability systems can also be constructed at the domain level, so that communities of organizations agree about appropriate standards, practices, and relations with key stakeholders.

While organizational accountability systems focus on the strategies and activities of individual organizations, domain accountability systems require interorganizational negotiations to define standards for community members. Often domain expectations about legitimacy and accountability are developed out of the experiences of their members, so agreement on standards and practices emerges from past practice. Domain standards may become embedded in wider social norms and legal standards, and so evolve into societal ideals of legitimacy and accountability embedded in laws, norms and expectations.

Interorganizational domains take many forms. For example, much of the attention on increasing the legitimacy and accountability of civil society organizations has focused on domains that involve organizations from the same sector. Members of sector domains carry out similar activities and have similar stakes in creating standards of legitimacy and accountability, such as the members of the development NGO sector in the Philippines.

A second important domain for civil society organizations is interorganizational campaigns to influence powerful actors like governments, corporations, and intergovernmental organizations. Campaigns may involve a wide range of concerned actors, such as the civil society organizations from local, national and international levels that have campaigned to stop dam building in India and Brazil. A third form of interorganizational domain is focused on a problem whose solution requires resources from many actors. Such problem domains may require standards based on legitimacy and accountability expectations negotiated across sectors and levels, such as the World Commission on Dams which was created to assess experience with large dams and define future standards and practices. Problem domains may require extended efforts to manage relations within the domain as well as with external stakeholders.

Constructing domain legitimacy and accountability systems requires (1) defining the domain and its stakeholders, (2) negotiating standards, codes and performance measures, (3) creating domain implementation organizations, and (4) enabling performance consequences for domain actors and stakeholders. Each of these elements is considered briefly below, and illustrated with experiences from around the world. Defining a domain requires that its members perceive common interests that justify both a substantial investment of time and energy and the loss of organizational autonomy from creating new standards.

Part of domain definition is building recognition among domain members that domain definition and collective action is in their interest. An initial question is who is inside and who is outside this domain, and how will it advance members' interests to participate. For the Philippine Council on NGO Certification (PCNC), for example, an important early question was whether NGOs with few or no deductible contributions had any interest in the tax reform that threatened those contributions. The domain would have been much smaller if they had decided not to join the alliance of CSOs dependent on such contributions from businesses or wealthy individuals.

The domain definition process also requires clarifying the nature, interests and priority of external stakeholders. Who are the stakeholders that affect or are affected by the domain's value creation activities? What stakeholders are important to the longer term legitimacy and support for the domain as a whole? External stakeholders for the PCNC domain, for example, included international donors, the business community, other government agencies and the general public concerned about the development roles of civil society in the Philippines.

While similarities and interdependencies of domain members may be easy to recognize intellectually, it is often difficult to mobilize members' resources for collective action. It is unlikely that civil society actors in the Philippines would have organized PCNC in the absence of the threat to civil society resources posed by fraudulent NGOs and the proposed tax reform. So, internal and eternal threats may be critical to catalysing domain definition initiatives.

The creation of clearer standards for a sector domain is often a consequence of external criticism of the activities of prominent sector members. The efforts to create shared standards for US child sponsorship NGOs. While leaders of some of those NGOs had been discussing shared standards and enhanced accountability for many years, serious commitment to developing those standards was generated by a media exposé that threatened their access to donors.

Leaders of the child sponsorship NGOs found that negotiating shared principles and standards helped their organizations learn from one another as well as protect themselves from arbitrary performance standards from outside critics. They also built relationships that could be used for alliances on other topics in the future. The utilization of a respected independent agency with a long track record in assessing the social impacts of businesses and other agencies helped to establish the credibility of the certification process.

Building accountability systems for civil society campaigns can be complicated by the need to include diverse allies. Campaign success often depends on articulating shared strategies and accountabilities for implementing them across large differences in interest and perspective. Interorganizational domains seldom have well-developed shared authority structures and civil society organizations often place high value on organizational autonomy. But civil society campaigns to influence powerful actors— governments, corporations, international agencies—require coalitions that can respond quickly to implement campaign strategies and tactics, and in some cases develop ways to protect their members when they seek to influence opponents unwilling to abide by the rule of law.

Some challenges involved in defining accountabilities in the civil society campaign to challenge human rights violations in Peru. Peru, rural branches (often in the most danger) had difficulty influencing national In decisions. The Coordinadora created an Executive Committee with more rural members and required that the Committee make decisions by consensus to preserve coalition cohesiveness and accountability to rural members. The Coordinadora also built relations with international supporters and other sectors of Peruvian civil society to enhance their influence in challenging both the Shining Path and authoritarian governments.

Bringing domain members together to build common strategies, standards and accountability expectations becomes more difficult as the diversity and conflict within the domain increase and as the dangers from outside stakeholders increase. The higher the tensions among members, the more concern with legitimacy and accountability and the more resources and time required to build agreements on domain strategy and performance expectations.

It was not easy to build shared standards among the child sponsorship organizations, which had histories of competing with each other. It was more difficult to construct shared strategies and tactics across differences among potential Coordinadora members, particularly when agents of external stakeholders like Shining Path revolutionaries sought to become members so they could focus attention on government human rights violations and away from their own abuses.

He external stakeholders for campaign alliances may include targets of the campaign, T such as the Government of Peru and Shining Path, other potential allies or opponents, and the general public. The Coordinadora campaign, for example, benefited from widespread international concern about human rights violations in Peru.

6

Government Financing and Accountability of NGOs

When developing a system for NGO financing, it is necessary to think through the underlying rationale and principles or assumptions on the part of the government. What is the role of NGOs in society? How is this role envisaged from the point of view of government? What roles and functions should government support and why? Below is a chart reflecting one potential classification, based on the principles and approaches generally described in Section III. It needs to be understood that:

- this is a generalized model and should be applied to fit the specifics of the country; and
- this is an idealized model, and roles of NGOs and types of support can in reality never be so clear.

Government Apply

Let's take the first box: NGOs undertaking governmental tasks (e.g., those explicitly assigned to central or local government in laws). Let's say the government believes that if an NGO undertakes a given task, it should be supported from the public budget because it is helping the government to do its job. How will it provide the support? The government may here choose from a range of principle-based mechanisms described above, such as the subsidiarity principle (preferring NGOs) or the competitive principle (looking for best value) as well as the normative or the voucher system. The questions of *what types of costs and to what extent they will be covered* are important, because if the government actually pays the whole cost to the NGO, it may not be worth privatizing the service in the first place.

Experience in the U.K. and Germany shows that NGOs fully subsidized by the government for a longer period (5 to 10 years) essentially became too expensive, like government agencies. Similarly, principles for each box should be well thought through. For NGOs in the second and third boxes, for example, the general principle may be that they will have the opportunity only to receive direct government funding if their current activities are in line with some specific government objective, and therefore supporting them will contribute to advance a government program. However, *indirect support* can be envisaged for all categories of NGOs at varying levels.

Usually, mutual benefit ones may enjoy only minimal support in recognition of their contribution to a democratic social model. This minimum could be the exemption on the corporate income tax for their statutory activities; it could, however, also include exemptions on duties and fees as well as property and other taxes (as in Hungary). NGOs that are considered public benefit would then enjoy a wider scale of benefits, such as the ability to receive tax-deductible donations, tax benefits regarding the income from economic activities, customs exemptions, ability to provide tax-exempt scholarships/aid to individuals, etc. In Hungary, two levels of PBOs enjoy additional benefits as "outstanding" PBOs; by contrast, in Bulgaria, MBOs do not even receive full exemption on the basic income tax (however, they do receive some tax exemptions – on grants and membership dues, for example).

Another issue is the 1% type tax allocation, which could be a benefit for all NGOs or just PBOs. The issue of *encouraging independent grantmaking* has also proved to be an important one in CEE countries, because as foreign donors withdraw and the culture of philanthropic giving has not yet developed, NGOs are left in a funding vacuum, where the only major source of support becomes the government. In light of this threat to financial sustainability, the establishment of local grantmakers is one potential solution. In the Czech Republic, the state actually supported endowing such grantmakers, but if such direct support is not an option, there are still instruments to help develop this potential (e.g., through regulating endowments and investments).

EUROPEAN GOVERNMENT POLICIES AND PRACTICES

Eastern European nonprofits have demonstrated extraordinary achievements during the past 10 to 15 years. Starting "from scratch" – a legal framework that either prohibited their existence or turned them into government satellites – they have played a remarkable role in the democratic processes that followed the fall of communism in this part of the world. Moreover, their participation in civil society development was a major contribution to the achievements in the economic, political, social, and cultural changes that brought about the accession of the new Eastern European members to the European Union. This, on the one hand, justified a "reward" on behalf of governments.

It called for government to support NGOs in each country for a better participation in the Union civil societal life, in political decision-making, and in the access to new financial sources. NGO expectations were naturally directed toward their more active role in formulating national positions on EU matters. For that, NGOs needed to develop additional capacity and to acquire new skills appropriate to the new political circumstances, new funding requirements, and new partnership opportunities. On the other hand, a continued and intensified involvement of the Third Sector in the various aspects of the accession process seemed only logical, because governments could benefit even further from civil society participation input.

In addition to governments' interest in such involvement, such an approach would be fully in line with the most recent European tendencies for expanding the mechanisms for social dialogue and public participation in EU decision-making. NGOs had much to offer during the accession process; however, they had much to ask for as well, and their cooperation with national governments was challenged in new ways. These challenges did not always lead to improved cooperation. Certain positive actions were taken – for example, NGO representatives were invited to participate in consultative meetings with EU institutions (Estonia), or received training on EU funding access (Czech Republic).

But not all available means were used to prepare national NGOs for EU public life and to support them in the new aspects of their struggle for a more active role or, in some cases, for existence and sustainability. This section outlines the various possible aspects of governmental positions regarding NGO participation in the accession process. It examines government policies and practices to support NGOs during the accession process in three ways: involving NGOs in EU decision-making, helping NGOs access EU funds (and co-financing), and providing direct (financial and institutional) help to NGOs to increase their viability and wider participation in EU life.

NGO Empowerment Part of Policy

The government's general attitude toward the importance of NGOs in the accession process varies greatly from country to country. For example, the Estonian government was strongly aware of the need to enhance civil society development. In April 2002, the government formed the *Estonian Joint Consultative Committee,* whose primary responsibility was to assist the accession process and prepare civil society organizations to enter the European Union. The Committee had wide representation – its members were designated by trade and industry sectors (the Estonian Chamber of Commerce and Industry), employers (the Estonian Confederation of Employers (ETTK), trade unions (the Estonian Employees' Unions' Association (TALO), the Confederation of Estonian Trade Unions (EAKL)), farmers (the Estonian Farmers Federation), and the NGO sector (Network of Estonian Nonprofit Organizations (NENO). The Joint Committee fosters dialogue and cooperation on the economic and social aspects of implementation of the European Agreement. Significantly less governmental assistance was extended to *Polish* nonprofits.

Polish NGOs were disappointed to witness the

government's passive attitude in accessing funds that could later be distributed to organized civil society. It is the government's responsibility to negotiate, apply for, and manage such funds, although the total amount will also depend on the third sector's capacity as estimated by the EU fund-allocating institutions. Polish NGOs need to learn how to access these funds and how to identify partners for participation in major projects. This is even more urgent given the fact that EU funds will be less available for Polish NGOs after the accession. While NGOs did receive substantial help from EU institutions and from European Nonprofit networks, they did not benefit significantly from their government's support in capacity-building, learning, partner-search, and available funds. Only in a few countries did the government actually document its commitment to involve NGOs in the preparation for accession in any substantial way.

The Czech Republic offers a concrete and outstanding example. The accession process has given the Czech government an opportunity to develop a specific form of partnership as one of its policies. It is part of the national development program and sectoral operational programs for using the Structural Funds. Although the government does not co-finance the projects submitted under these funds and does not give advance grants, it has established an efficient political and institutional system which assists NGOs as beneficiaries of EU funds. The NGO sector is involved in the process of economic and social cohesion through their representative in the Steering and Coordinating Committee– the leading coordinating body in that field. The NGO representative is nominated by the Governmental Council for Non-governmental Nonprofit Organizations. *The National Development Plan* is the fundamental document for all operational programs.

The plan is developed under the auspices of the Ministry for Regional Development. The public participation in the drafting process is ensured through public discussions and workshops held on the separate chapters. The NGO sector is actively represented in and contributes to these discussions. On that basis, several operational programs have been drafted and implemented under the competence of the separate ministries. They permitted NGOs operating in a given area to participate in the preparation of the ministry's "action plans" for the development of that area and to have improved access to EU funding provided for the same purpose.

For example, the *Joint Regional Operational Programme ("JROP")* was drafted as a multi-fund program for the European Regional Development Fund and for the European Social Fund within the remit of the Ministry for Regional Development. The Commission for Regional Development was constituted as a basic coordinating body responsible for the preparation of measures concerning regional policies. The Nonprofit sector has been represented in the Commission as well as in six of the eight working groups established by the Ministry that drafted the Program. The Program identifies several priority areas in which support should be provided to NGOs. These include "Local development of human resources; Improving the environment in municipalities and regions; Revival of rural areas; and Development of tourism in municipalities and regions."

Another operational Program, *Objective 2 for the Prague Cohesion Region,* was drafted under the competence of the Ministry for Regional Development for purposes of utilization of the European Regional Development Fund by the City of Prague. Under that document, support from the European Regional

Development Fund is allocated to NGOs. At the same time, the cooperation principle is ensured through the participation of the civil sector in the Commission of the Prague Cohesion Region Council, following a mechanism similar to that applied under JROP.

Following a similar pattern, NGOs have also been involved in preparing several other programs, which allow them to benefit from EU funds. Among these programs are the following:

- *The Human Resources Development Operational Programme and Single Programming Document for Objective 3 of the Prague cohesion region* drafted within the Ministry of Labour and Social Affairs and offering NGOs an access to the European Social Fund;
- *The Development of Rural Areas and multifunctional agriculture* prepared and implemented by the Ministry of Agriculture and assisting NGOs to utilize the financial resources of the European Agriculture Guidance and Guarantee Fund. According to that program, a local strategy group must be established, with the purpose of drafting a strategy for local development. The group should also take responsibility for implementing that strategy. In order to accomplish their task successfully, the strategy groups must reflect a well-balanced representation of all stakeholders in the given area; therefore, NGOs are envisaged as partners in that process.
- *The Operational Programme Environment* prepared by the Ministry of Environment, including NGOs as beneficiaries of the financing from the European Regional Development Fund. The partnership

principle for this program is being pursued by having representatives of NGOs included in the implementation structure, in particular as members of the monitoring committee. NGOs also participate in preparing the strategic environmental assessment.

During the preparation of the programmatic documents concerning the access to the Structural Fund, representatives of Czech NGOs drafted and submitted their comments. Fourteen regional roundtables were organized and NGOs working in the respective regions had the opportunity to comment on the documents. The roundtables served as an excellent potential source of feedback that reached the authors of the programming documents. However, the lack of a well-established, working mechanism for submitting comments and remarks posed a barrier that prevented the proper delivery and use of the comments. If such a system had been applied at the national level, it would have ensured that the necessary space for participation and consultation was provided to representatives of NGOs.

GOVERNMENT SUPPORT TO NGOS

It was widely recognized in accession countries that NGOs needed to strengthen their organizational capacities in order to be able to access pre-accession and especially post-accession financing sources. Strengthening organizational capacity may include training sessions on project planning and proposal writing as well as educating NGOs on how the EU works and how they can participate in EU-wide networks for policy advocacy. Moreover, government support for general organizational development, e.g., helping to introduce quality assurance systems for service-providing NGOs, was also a demonstrated need. However, apart from the inclusion of such activities in the PHARE and other pre-accession grant mechanisms, governments have done little to increase the capacity of the NGO sector in comparison to the investment made in developing the capacity of enterprises.

Where there have been such examples, they occurred as a result of the initiative of the individual government agencies or public officials and not as a consequence of a coordinated public policy. For example, NGOs in the Czech Republic have been trained on the procedures for application for EU funding; however, this effort was not part of the government's global policy on EU accession or on civil society support and was realized through separate state agencies. A more positive example could be cited from *Hungary*, where the government launched a so-called *Proposal Preparation Fund*, which provides technical assistance specifically to local governments, small-region associations, and Nonprofit organizations. Those organizations that aim to apply to the EU Structural Funds were given the opportunity to send an idea to the Fund. The Fund then provided the necessary means to develop the awarded ideas into full-fledged project proposals, which stood greater chances of securing EU funding. In 2003, the Proposal Preparation Fund awarded close to 500 applicants, including local governments and civil organizations, technical assistance worth a total of 27 million Euros. For the 2003 round, the government and the PHARE program both contributed 50% to the Fund; based on the success of this initiative (they received more than 2,800 ideas), the government decided to launch the program again in 2004 at the same level of support, even without the PHARE contribution.

Financial Means

Not only are national financing and co-financing mechanisms essential for NGOs' sustainability in general; they may also be a requirement for access to EU funds. The structure of these mechanisms has been used for the distribution of external funding. For example, in the *Czech Republic*, the pre-accession assistance provided by the EU under the Accession Partnerships and pre-accession financial mechanisms were administered under a separate Program of Civil Society Development and through the Foundation for Development of Civil Society. The Foundation was based in Prague and was established for this purpose on the initiative of the Czechoslovak Federal Government in 1992. A total of EUR 16,770,000 was distributed under the Program by the end of 2001. The Estonian Joint Consultative Committee created in 2002 had concluded that *Estonia* needed to develop such financing mechanisms.

They were necessary not only to improve the level of information regarding pre-accession issues and access to Structural Funds but also to establish a national co-financing system and to ensure NGO involvement in the discussion and adoption of funding solutions. The *Hungarian* government chose another way of addressing the need to strengthen NGOs financially at the doorstep of the EU.

While the role or importance of NGOs was not explicitly mentioned in the National Development Plan and the consequent policy papers, the Hungarian government emphasized the importance of supporting NGOs in the accession process in its Governmental Strategy Towards the Civil Sector. The National Civil Fund, set up to strengthen the NGO sector has established a special college (grant-giving body) to support efforts of NGOs in positioning themselves and the sector in the accession process. In addition, national efforts should be backed up by EU preparatory work. The European Commission should help not only civil servants but also civil society organizations to acquire knowledge of the Structural Funds. Civil society organizations should, for their part, make efficient use of Structural Funds resources in the future and carry out effective preparatory work so as to be ready for the co-financing and management of the projects concerned. The Commission provides support to a number of *European-wide NGO networks* in order to promote this function, which in turn reach out and educate NGOs in accession countries in European matters. Among these organizations are the European Citizen Action Service, the European Council for Voluntary Organisations, and the TRIALOG project.

NGO FINANCIAL VIABILITY

In this baseline year for the NGO Sustainability Index for Sub-Saharan Africa, a number of positive elements are evident in the country reports. NGOs' ability to provide life-saving service delivery to under-served populations was the highest score in all 19 countries. While service delivery appears to be a strength, financial viability is a weakness. Across all country reports, the scores for financial viability ranked the lowest among the seven indicators. A common issue for many NGOs is reliance on a single, external source for funding. In this situation, if international funding were to disappear, many of the NGOs would collapse. While this financial weakness may reflect the overall economic situation in many countries which are themselves heavily dependent on international aid, there are several examples from various reports where

NGOs and donors are exploring innovative approaches to supporting NGOs.

Across the 19 country reports, the narrative section on financial viability consistently delivered the message that many NGOs depend on international donors with limited availability of support from local sources such as government and individual and corporate philanthropy. This description could just as easily have been written in 2000 or 1990.

These narrative discussions are supplemented by the data generated from the analysis and scoring of each country by the Expert Panels who jointly determine the NGO sector's rating on the financial viability dimension of the NGO Sustainability Index for Sub-Saharan Africa (NGOSI). Some of the highlights and findings from this data review include:

- Of the 19 countries studied, five, (e.g., Kenya, Tanzania, South Africa, Mozambique and Senegal), were in the second of three stages of financial viability, "sustainability evolving"; the remaining 14 were in the "sustainability impeded" stage; and no country met the criteria for "sustainability enhanced", the first stage. What do the five countries that scored highest in financial viability have in common? Except for Mozambique, each of the other four countries has well established NGO sectors, among the oldest on the continent with mature and diverse NGOs. All five countries except Rwanda rate relatively high on a democracy index with freedoms of association, assembly and speech largely respected by concerned governments. In relative terms, these countries would be considered to have economies that surpass the norm in the region and thus make local resource mobilization more likely although not enough to achieve the highest stage of financial viability.

- South Africa with the best overall score is also the country with the greatest diversification of its resource base and with the highest percentage of funding coming from government. This is an indication that government values NGO participation in national development and those NGOs have strong capabilities to bid on and win government contracts and grants.
- Conversely, the five countries with the lowest scores, i.e., Gabon, Zimbabwe, Angola, Guinea and Burundi, tend to have either relatively young NGO sectors or public policies and legal frameworks that have not favoured the development of civil society. All five countries rank at or near the bottom in most social and economic indicators of the United Nations Development Program's Human Development Index despite, in the case of Angola and Gabon, immense mineral wealth.
- Conflict and post-conflict countries such as the Democratic Republic of Congo (DRC), Sierra Leone, Liberia, Zimbabwe, and Guinea scored nearly as low as the five countries at the bottom of the rankings. However, in the case of both Liberia and Sierra Leone, there appears to be a positive movement as the two countries consolidate more democratic systems of governance and provide NGOs with a relatively more sound enabling environment.

While the reports offer some encouraging news about NGO funding, including new and innovative resource mobilization strategies and approaches, it is also clear that NGO financial viability still has far to go. As this is the base-line year for the NGOSI, it is important to examine case studies of higher levels of financial viability for NGOs. The NGOSI is based upon the premise that the NGO sector develops along a continuum. Therefore, this paper will explore many approaches to financial viability, and try to learn from and apply examples of good practice as well as significant innovations in this field.

NGO FUNDING AND DEVELOPMENT IN AFRICA

There are several major historical markers that have helped to define the way in which the NGO sector in the 19 countries covered by this Index has evolved and developed into what it is today, including its ability to sustain itself financially. The first such historical marker was the prolonged drought of the early 1970s, which devastated the Sahel and the Horn of Africa, Ethiopia in particular. This drought was important because it brought the first wave of so-called Northern NGOs to Africa, funded primarily by Northern governments and private citizens. These organizations responded to the humanitarian crisis at that time, and many remain today. Some might argue that the local NGOs which emerged were essentially created in the image of their Northern NGOs counterparts.

The second major influence on the development of the NGO sector in many countries in the region was the structural adjustment programs (SAPs), imposed by international financial institutions and implemented by governments during the 1980s. SAPs essentially forced governments to withdraw from the provision of public services (e.g., education, health) or suffer the consequences:

primarily a halt to western loans and credits for economies already on the brink following years of corruption and mismanagement. At the same time, SAPs created space for new, indigenous and secular NGOs to address social and economic problems that had been growing in the years following independence. This space was further opened by donors who wanted to replace government-as-the-engine-of-economic-growth with the private sector. As the decade progressed NGOs took over from government the delivery of public services, to a considerable degree in some countries. This period saw an introduction of a new funding mechanism for African NGOs: the Private Voluntary Organization (PVO) Umbrella Support Mechanism.

The third event that had a major impact on the NGO sector's financial viability was the democratization movement that began in the early 1990s. Benin's Sovereign National Conference, which took place in February 1990, is often viewed as the beginning of the many national democratic transitions that marked the decade and that were characterized by the participation of civil society organizations.

After 1990, there was an explosion of autonomous, voluntary associations representing their citizen-members' interests and aspirations. Organizations that may have been little more than appendages of the government or a political party (e.g., chambers of commerce, women's and youth leagues, cooperatives, bar associations) became independent and capable of more effectively representing their members' and constituents' interests. Some of these organizations adopted democratic governance structures, with broad-based membership. There were some that created federated bodies to engage with government at all levels, thereby extending members' and constituents' voices to the centers of power where public policy decisions were made.

The implications of this development for civil society in terms of financing are several-fold:

- First, a far greater and more diverse group of organizations was now competing for funding, much of it from external donors, including international NGOs, and their respective governments;
- Second, new areas of programmatic intervention were added post-1990 and principally the democracy and governance sector, which included such areas as human rights promotion, conflict management, accountability, transparency, and advocacy;
- Third, more funding from donors was committed to the support of civil society, particularly to strengthen organizational capacity; and
- Finally, community-based organizations figured into many civil society strategies in light of their legitimacy and potential ability to self-finance their activities. Traditional associations, such as Tontines, and natural resource users groups, and more modern social and economic groups, such as the groupes d'interet economique, cooperatives, and parent-teacher associations, gained increased scrutiny by donors and local research institutions. Continued Challenges to Financial Viability

Many NGOs in Sub-Saharan Africa continue to struggle with the effects of donor funding decisions on their structure and direction. Another major challenge is the reluctance of many governments to accept NGOs as full partners in development and democratic governance.

At this point in the history of international development, most Sub-Saharan African governments depend on donor funding for significant portions of their national budgets. To give an extreme example, approximately 80 percent of Rwanda's health budget is funded by its development partners.

Several of the countries reviewed by the NGOSI are not only low-income but are emerging from violent conflict (e.g., Liberia, Sierra Leone, Rwanda); have ongoing conflict (e.g., DRC, Uganda); or, they have the potential for violent conflict to reignite (Zimbabwe, Guinea). Few beneficiaries, NGOs or donors are inclined to focus on the financial viability of NGOs factors when they are preoccupied by short-term humanitarian needs and vulnerable populations. This point was clearly brought out in the country reports on Sierra Leone, Zimbabwe and DRC, among others, where NGOs have been heavily relied upon to provide emergency relief services.

Donors are an important part of this discussion of NGO financial viability, and they should consider how their activities and beneficiaries could have significant and often unintended consequences for civil society. As discussed earlier, donor choices made during the 1980s and 1990s had a major impact on the structure, differentiation and capacity of NGOs in Sub-Saharan Africa. The country reports note many examples of successful NGO resource mobilization yet many challenges remain. For example, many governments view NGOs with distrust, illustrated by the fact that few country reports cited NGO access or success in competing for government contracts. It would be useful to examine the sources of this distrust in greater depth in order to understand how this key issue can be resolved in different country contexts.

This paper has provided some insights into NGO financial viability, offering relevant examples of good practices and strategies for resource mobilization. Significantly, there exists a broad array of organizations representing the diversity of associational life found in many Sub-Saharan African countries today. Despite the manifold challenges confronting them, many of these organizations have proven resilient and dynamic in periods of great financial hardship. As they pursue funding sources, it is important that they seek diverse and sustainable sources, both local and external, to the maximum extent possible. The NGO Sustainability Index is a new resource to aid in the sharing of information, experiences and lessons among development stakeholders, promoting NGO financial sustainability in Sub-Saharan Africa and in other regions of the world.

DEMOCRATIC ACCOUNTABILITY

The idea that it is good for organizations and people to be more accountable is widespread in many societies, even if the word does not translate well into all languages (Lister, 2003). There is a wide variety of definitions of accountability used or assumed by people working on questions of organizational transparency, responsiveness, ethics, legitimacy and regulation, whether in relation to governments, corporations, NGOs or other organizations (Bakker, 2002). When we use the term accountability we can break it down into four questions: who is accountable, to whom, for what and how? If we look at how these questions have been answered by different organizations and individuals, immediately problems arise with the assumption that accountability is necessarily a good thing. 'I was just following orders' is an often heard refrain at war crimes trials from Nuremberg to present day scandals in Iraq and elsewhere. Repressive regimes often have very thorough systems of accountability. People's devotion to a specific group and its leaders and the unquestioning following of orders are all aspects of accountability that have facilitated some of the worst atrocities in the history of humankind. So accountability is not a good thing in itself and a lack of accountability is not necessarily a bad thing, particularly in societies that tend towards the centralization of power and autocracy. Is there a particular form of accountability that merits being regarded as desirable?

We argue that the answer to this question lies in a deep understanding of rights and democracy. The basic idea of demos kratos, or people rule, is that people govern themselves. In a democratically-governed society, a community of people ideally has meaningful participation in decisions and processes that affect them and is not systematically adversely affected by another group of people without being able to rectify the situation (Dahl, 1961; Isbister, 2001). Organizations of all forms, not just governmental, influence people's lives. The concept of 'stakeholder' can be useful here as it groups together people on the basis of their being affected by an organization. Because the demos that make claims for the democratic control (directly or indirectly) of organizations are those affected by the organizations, this can be understood as 'stakeholder democracy'. Stakeholder democracy can be defined as an ideal system of governance of a society where all stakeholders in an organization or activity have the same opportunity to govern that organization or activity (Bendell, 2005). With these concepts in mind, the ideal is a society where all decisionmaking is accountable to those affected by those decisions or indecisions. This ideal of democratic accountability is one that concerns the whole of society, not just a particular organization. However, for this principle to be workable for the management and regulation of organizations, our challenge is to identify a form of accountability for individual organizations that is constitutive of this broader societal democratic accountability.

The principle of democratic accountability means that a mining company should be more accountable to people poisoned downstream from one of its mines. It does not mean poisoned communities downstream from the mining company need be accountable to the mining company. This highlights how the accountability of individual organizations to those they affect is sometimes facilitative of the goal of more democratically accountable decision-making in society, but not always. If an NGO articulating the interests of the poisoned community had to be more accountable to the mining company, or perhaps a government that was strongly influenced by that company, this relationship would not necessarily increase the democratic accountability of decisionmaking in that context.

A real world example highlights this issue clearly. Recently there have been calls for advocacy NGOs to be accountable to those organizations they campaign on (Vibert, 2003). One NGO coalition called 'Fifty Years is Enough' criticizes the policies and programmes of the World Bank on behalf of its 200 member organizations. The World Bank manages over US$25 billion a year, with a paid staff of over 8000. 'Fifty Years is Enough' has three paid staff and a very tight budget.

This NGO has an implicit accountability to the World Bank, in the sense that it would be quickly criticized if it made mistakes with its basic facts and figures and have to explain itself. Promoting greater organizational accountability of this small NGO to all those affected by its work, such as the World Bank, and with the resources this process would require, would not help promote the accountability of decision-making to those affected by decisions in the field it works on. Promoting organizational accountability as a whole may not promote the accountability of decisionmaking processes to the people whose lives they influence. The relative power of different organizations must be taken into account in our understanding of the accountability challenge.

This understanding of democratic accountability does not make the accountability of NGOs less important. Rather, it means that NGOs should be accountable to those they affect who have less power. To use the hypothetical mining example, if an NGO engaged with a community affected by a mine was successful in stopping the mining company from poisoning its river, but in doing so the company diverted its pollution towards other rivers and communities, the accountability of that NGO to the newly affected communities would become an issue.

The implication is that we need to consider social systems, rather than just organizational units within those systems. The accountability of one part of a system helps to create a more democratically accountable system if it is accountable to those parts affected by its decisions/ actions that have less power and that are accountable to other parts of the system in the same way. Democratic accountability can be described by answering the four accountability questions as follows:

1 Who is accountable? The person or group that affects some relatively less powerful person or group.

2 To whom? To the person or group they are affecting.

3 For what? For the effect they have on them, particularly if it is negative.

4 How? In a way whereby the person or group affected can change the behaviour of the person or group affecting them (with the affected also becoming accountable to any third parties they affect when exerting this influence).

These are simple principles concerning individual organizational units in our infinitely complex and interconnected social system, and are therefore fallible and provide only a guide. The principles include recognition that ever wider circles of interconnection between organizations are crucial to whether the relationships between organizations at the centre of that circle are as constitutive of democracy as possible. The importance of the accountability of these wider relationships does not mean that an organization can claim it will not be accountable to a relatively less powerful organization unless that organization is itself accountable to other less powerful organizations or people. To continue with the hypothetical, the mining company should not require that an NGO working with a community affected by the mine be accountable to all other stakeholders before the company will be accountable to that NGO. However, in recognizing the wider connections, it would be beneficial for the company to encourage that NGO to consider its own accountability to those it could influence by reaching agreement with the mining company.

A key issue that is raised by this definition of democratic accountability concerns how we know which organizations have more or less power. Power is a concept that has been explored in detail by sociologists for decades

(Clegg, 1989), and although this work needs to inform policy and practice in this area, it is beyond the scope of this chapter. For our purposes, proxies for power can be found in property and force: those with more property are more powerful, as are those with more ability to use force, such as governments (who are meant to have a monopoly on the use of force in a society). Many commentators on accountability emphasize 'placing a check on the authority of the powerful' to the extent that 'in common usage... "accountability" is shorthand for democratic accountability - accountability to ordinary people and to the legal framework through which governance is affected' (Goetz and Jenkins, 2002). This is also implicit in the distinctions many people make between a people's or organization's upward accountability to donors or governments, or others with power over them, and downward accountability to those affected by them. By developing this implicit idea into an explicit concept of democratic accountability we seek to frame an agenda for donor accountability that supports the wider enjoyment of rights and the deepening of democracy.

In the following sections, we describe how different types of donors have important democratic accountability deficits within their current practice. We then outline a set of principles for democratic donor accountability, relate these to current initiatives on donor accountability and make recommendations for further work.

DEMOCRATIC ACCOUNTABILITY DEFICITS IN CURRENT DONOR PRACTICE

Government Donors

Government aid agencies that act as donors are accountable to the state they serve. Bilateral aid agencies have their overarching strategies and priorities developed by the politicians in government and must report back to often multiple arms of that government. The wholesale cutting back of the Danish bilateral aid agency after a change in government illustrates how this form of accountability is decisive. Intergovernmental donors (and lenders), such as the World Bank and the IMF, are primarily accountable to the governments that finance them. Consequently, the countries of Europe and North America have the most influence over these institutions. These forms of accountability can conflict with a broader conception of democratic accountability, where funders would be responsive to those in most need.

Historical and contemporary geopolitics mean government-to-government aid has not gone to those countries that need it most. Israel receives over US$2 billion a year in military aid and about US$600 million dollars in economic assistance from the US. In addition, much governmental aid is either explicitly tied or effectively allocated to companies based in the donor country. The same is true with NGOs, with governments often giving to those based in their own countries rather than directly to Southern organizations. Even emergency humanitarian aid has often been 'driven by political interests rather than according to need' (Harmer and Cotterrell, 2004). The tying of aid may also reflect other motivations such as religious values. The first administration of George W. Bush and its restrictive policy (popularly known as the Global Gag Rule) on giving to organizations providing resources or services linked to abortion is one such example (Centre for Reproductive Rights, 2003).

There are also accountability issues surrounding the influence that government donors (especially Northern ones) have through their funding of NGOs. Many governments in the global south are uneasy about their lack of control over organizations funded almost entirely by foreign interests. Some governmental concerns may arise from a desire to suppress democracy and centralize power, as has been suggested to be the government's aim in Colombia (War on Want, 2003). However, there is a significant issue about the influence of foreign-funded groups on domestic culture, economics and politics, especially where the concept of development is contested and hard to attain. One controversial example of NGOs being used as subcontractors to fulfill a government donor foreign policy agenda comes from Iraq. In 2003, the Research Triangle Institute (RTI), an NGO involved in drug research, became heavily involved in the occupation of Iraq. RTI undertook a 'local governance' contract from the US government worth around US$466 million. 'It turns out that the town councils RTI has been setting up are the centerpiece of Washington's regional caucuses - a plan that has been so widely rejected in Iraq' (Klein, 2004). Under the friendly rubric of capacity building and local partnerships, Klein contends that RTI was playing its part in the creation of a US-appointed government that could then make or confirm a range of decisions on international agreements, privatization and IMF loans that would effectively handcuff future democratically elected governments. Therefore, it is not just the accountability of NGOs that can be questioned, but also the selectivity by which donors fund NGOs and the real commitment that donors have to increase citizens' participation through the medium of NGOs.

The lack of a commonly understood approach to international development assistance means that it is difficult to hold governments to account for their overseas aid programmes. Two key intergovernmental commitments provide something of a benchmark for assessing the accountability of government aid activities. The first concerns the amount of support. In the 1970s, donor-nation governments committed to contribute 0.7 per cent of their GDP to overseas aid (Bissio, 2003). In 2002, only 5 of the 22 reporting countries were meeting this target (German and Randell, 2004). The second concerns the intended development objectives of the donors. In 2000, countries agreed to the Millennium Development Goals (MDGs), which include a commitment to halve those living in poverty by 2015. While processes for monitoring developing countries commitments and progress have been institutionalized, systems for monitoring the performance of donors are only beginning to be put into place (UNDP, 2003). It is worth noting that the first goal, which sought gender equity in primary education, was already missed by some distance in 2005. No donors were held to account. Tied aid, increasing levels of poverty and problems with the MDGs illustrate the challenge of establishing and then promoting an agenda for government donors to become more accountable to the people they claim to help.

Corporate Donors

When corporations give away finance, products or staff time, they must do so in accordance with the governance of their organization. In the case of privately owned companies, the nature of corporate giving is dependent on the individual owners involved. For publicly traded companies, in most countries corporate law indicates that shareholders' interests must be paramount in the managers' considerations. Ultimately, reports to shareholders will encompass all corporate activities, including sponsorships and donations.

The strength of these forms of accountability is questioned by some shareholder groups, who believe managers have too much freedom. This form of accountability is much more explicit than democratic accountability, which would encompass all those a corporation affects through the conduct of its business. Corporate funding of NGOs has grown significantly in recent years (Common Dreams, 2003). Some of this is straightforward sponsorship aimed at very explicit marketing and advertising objectives.

For example, in 1999, the tobacco multinational giant Philip Morris 'spent US$75 million on charitable contributions, and US$100 million to publicize these donations' (National Council on Responsive Philanthropy, 2005). Corporations sometimes donate money in order to influence public opinion in ways essential for brand confidence and loyalty.

When health charity the Arthritis Foundation agreed to put its name to McNeil Consumer Products in exchange for a donation that totaled US$2 million, the company marketed aspirin and other common drugs under the Arthritis Foundation's name. McNeil was sued for a US$2 million settlement in 1996 for implying that the products were new medications created by the foundation. The Attorney General involved said 'when a nonprofit's credibility is sold for profit, the public has a right to know who's behind the name, what's inside the product, and where the money is going' (Centre for Science in the Public Interest, 2003).

The way that corporate donors may use their money to influence public perceptions is also an issue (Common Cause, 2005). But this goes deeper in ways firmly hidden from public view. For example, the US-based Society for

Women's Health Research (SWHR) criticized the National Institutes of Health for publicizing a major study that found hormone replacement therapy (HRT) increased risks of breast cancer and heart attacks. What concerned citizens hearing of SWHR criticisms would not have known is that Wyeth, a company that markets the most widely used HRT drug is a major donor to SWHR (Centre for Science in the Public Interest, 2003).

Research institutes and think tanks have become key recipients of corporate funds and this has become a concern where they have significant reach and influence in arenas of policy-making. Public Interest Watch (PIW) is one of a new breed of conservative watchdog organizations whose purpose ostensibly centers on calling for more NGO accountability.

PIW describes its mission as 'keeping an eye on the self-appointed guardians of the public interest' and lambastes non-profit hospitals in the US, saying they are grabbing huge amounts of public money that does not belong to them (PIW 2004). However, PIW is funded by companies including private healthcare providers whose interests are clearly manifest in PIW advocacy. The broader political interests of companies should also be remembered as factors that shape their philanthropy.

Many corporations establish foundations to organize their philanthropy. Funding for these can be raised by employee payroll giving schemes, or by donations from the corporate body itself. In most countries these foundations and the donations they receive are tax exempt. In return, the foundation is required to be operationally separate from the company (Common Dreams, 2003). However, in many cases the independence of these foundations can be questioned. The Shell Foundation, for example, is housed in the head offices of the oil company Shell, uses their information technology and administrative systems, has Shell employees on the board and secretariat and uses the same logo. Given this, it can be questioned why donations by these organizations often gain the same tax advantages as charitable gifts that do not enhance the position of a for-profit company.

Civil Donors

We consider four broad categories of donors in the civil sector: religious organizations, highly wealthy individuals, large intermediary NGOs and charitable foundations. Many religions inspire their followers to help other people, either directly or by providing funds. How that help is conceived depends on the particular religion, but it usually involves matters of basic welfare, such as food, clothing, shelter, healthcare and friendship, as well as the spiritual well-being of people.

Concerns arise with the way religious beliefs may influence access to, or the nature of, any help provided. In addition, questions can be raised about the appropriateness of some forms of religious proselytizing, particularly in relation to contemporary notions of rights and democracy, as well as the political agendas that can be incorporated into spiritual messages. These concerns have become more acute in recent years as the nation state is less involved in providing welfare services and has started cofunding the provision of welfare by religious institutions.

Different religious institutions have different forms of governance and different freedoms or restrictions from the state, so the accountability issues they pose are diverse. Some religious institutions are democratically accountable to their followers, such as the Baha'i World Community, whereas others are more centralized, like the Catholic Church. The view that a religious community is ultimately accountable to a divine being, rather than the people it affects throughout their lives, may at first seem to challenge democratic accountability.

However, most spiritual traditions explain that love for and service of others are the natural enactment of a spiritual consciousness, thus there need not be an inherent conflict at the level of principle. However, conflict at the level of practice is inevitable given the fallibility of any human and human institution, religious or otherwise. Highly wealthy individuals are another category of civil sector donors with powerful influence over the work of those they fund.

It may seem unnecessarily suspicious to question the accountability of a rich person only when they choose to dispose of their funds, but in a world where the 200 richest individuals have assets equivalent to the poorest half of humanity, the personal views of such donors can have a major impact on societies worldwide. In recent years questions have been raised about the practices and accountability of charitable foundations, particularly in relation to issues like high salaries, controversial grant-making and inefficient monitoring. Susan Berresford, the President of the Ford Foundation, has urged foundations to make their sector more accountable: 'We have a clear problem of public accountability right now, but we have routes ahead that can help us' (Berresford, 2004).

Tax breaks are a major source of revenue for foundations. Estimates put the total percentage of US foundation funds earned through tax breaks at around 45 per cent, which is money that comes from the American public (National Council on Responsive Philanthropy, 2005). Even when funding is from independent charitable foundations, not overtly directed by corporations, reflecting on where the money actually came from provides different insights into the question of accountability.

Many foundations are founded or funded by rich individuals, families or religious institutions and seek to give away money in the way that the founders request. A recipient of a donation from such a foundation may understandably feel some gratitude to the donor, and many recipients feel it is right to be accountable to that donor and to comply with the restrictions and expectations surrounding the donation. But we cannot ignore that the power of donors to be able to give comes from the endeavors and sometimes even the suffering of other people.

Consider the world's largest foundation. Its existence is a credit to the Gates benefactors, yet we should recognize how the funds originally came from Microsoft profits, which in turn came from the fact that employees of the firms in the global value chains making Microsoft products and services are paid less than those products and services are able to fetch, and that consumers of those products and services pay more than they cost to produce. This is not a specific criticism, since paying people less than the value of the products they produce is always how profit is derived.

The value of a foundation is then maintained through its investments in other companies pursuing the same profit-motivated approach. Therefore, any money coming from a foundation arises through the efforts of millions of people. This reminds us of the interconnections of endeavor and exploitation that generate the financial power that can then be reallocated through donations.

Donors could consider themselves accountable to those who generated the revenues as much as they might expect NGOs to be accountable to them as recipients of these same accumulations of societal wealth. Whole societies are responsible for generating such wealth and so a donor can be said to owe a broad debt to society as a whole. Procedural approaches to accountability can not easily deal with this complexity.

The implication is that our sense of interconnectedness and the humanistic values this sense arises from and informs are as important to democratic accountability as management procedures or a financial audit. We can keep this difficulty in mind when considering what policies and initiatives on donor accountability might prove helpful in promoting democratic accountability more broadly.

7

Financial Management: Grant-Writing and Budgeting

For most NGOs, grant-writing constitutes the largest portion of all fundraising efforts. Sources for grants include: (i) government agencies; (ii) corporations; (iii) private foundations; (iv) individuals; (v) international donors, such as the United Nations or USAID; and (vii) other NGOs. A grant proposal is a "statement of purpose that is presented for someone's acceptance ... [that] intends to persuade that person to fund your project." A proposal can be summed up as follows:

- It states the problem or challenge that the NGO seeks to address or resolve;
- It offers a plan with clearly stated goals, objectives, and strategies for solving the problem;
- It asks for specific financial or in-kind resources to accomplish the plan;
- It shows that you are capable of doing what you say you will; and

- According to specified measures that you have accomplished, it offers a pledge that you will be able to accomplish what you said you would.

In short, every proposal should answer who, what, when, where, why, and how about the project.

Writing a grant proposal, which can also be referred to as a project proposal, is a lengthy and time-consuming process. Therefore, it is necessary to allow as much time as possible to work on a proposal. Starting the process early will give you the time necessary to define your ideas clearly and share your drafts with colleagues who can provide valuable input and comments that will ensure that you submit an excellent proposal.

Research and Preparation

Before beginning your research on which grant providers might fund a proposal, you need to identify a problem that needs to be solved. For example:

- Rural Iraqi women do not have access to credit to start small businesses.

After you have an idea for the proposal, the next stage is to find grant opportunities that match your project goals and begin researching the required elements of a specific proposal.

For example, you can look for grants that provide funding or small grants to NGOs that will help rural women start small businesses. Do not limit your funding search to one source as there are many grants available for NGOs. When searching for potential donors, make sure that the proposal, mission, and objectives of your project match the donor's specifications.

In addition to matching the general purpose of the program to your potential donor, you will need to outline the specifics of the program (methods, timetable, and resources required), and a general budget; this information will allow you to narrow your search to potential donors whose grants match your needs. Once you have identified a grant suitable for your purposes, request the proposal guidelines (including content, format, and deadlines) from the source. Try to establish direct contact with the donors so that you can maintain an ongoing dialogue that will help you focus your efforts on what is most important for them. Although the main purpose of your project is to help your beneficiaries, you will also need to ensure that the project satisfies your donor's expectations. For budgeting purposes, you need to clarify the maximum amount of money available for the grant and determine whether it fits your needs.

In order to write a successful proposal, find and study other grant proposals that have been funded by the same organization so you can learn from the experience of other NGOs and determine what type of proposals are generally accepted by the funding source. Review your own past project proposals and project evaluations, both successful and unsuccessful, in order to analyse your strengths and weaknesses. (Knowing your strengths and weaknesses will enable you to design a project based on your strengths; moreover, donors will be more likely to fund an organization that has a strong tradition of monitoring and evaluation.) Verify any statistical data you will be using in your proposal to ensure its accuracy. Once you have all the necessary guidelines and background information you can begin writing your grant proposal.

Writing the Proposal

Once you have the materials for the specific proposal, you must follow all of the instructions found in the guidelines. These guidelines can be very detailed, so review them carefully before writing a proposal. As stated above, while proposal guidelines will vary, most of them include a variation of the components described below.

In general, the components of a proposal are as follows:

1. Cover Letter (Overview of funding request)
2. Cover Sheet (Abstract/Executive Summary)
3. Narrative Project Description/Work Plan:
   a. Needs Assessment
   b. Goals and Objectives
   c. Activities/Methodology
   d. Staffing/Administration
   e. Monitoring/Reporting/Evaluation
   f. Sustainability
4. Budget
5. Organization Biography and Background Information
6. Conclusion
7. Appendices.

Cover Letter

No longer than one page, a cover letter should give a clear and concise overview of the organization and the reason for the funding request. It sets forth how your proposal furthers the donor's mission, goals, and objectives, and meets the specific requirements of the proposal guidelines.

Abstract/Executive Summary

Although you may want to include a title page or a table of contents for longer proposals, the first substantive section is the abstract, sometimes referred to as an executive summary. The abstract is a brief, precise summary of your project. This first page is the most important section of the whole document as it sets forth the framework in easily understandable terms for the donor. Donors receive many grant proposals and do not have a lot of time to review them, so they first look at the abstract to determine if they should continue reading the proposal. Therefore, your abstract needs to persuade the reader that your proposal is a worthy project for his or her further attention and examination.

Specifically, an abstract does the following: 1) it identifies the community need and issues the project addresses; 2) outlines the solution the project offers and the impact on beneficiaries; 3) identifies the total financial and other resources needed; and 4) describes the organization and emphasizes its area of expertise and its ability to carry out the proposed program successfully.

Writing your abstract as the last step in the grant-writing process may be easier as you will be more familiar with the details of the project and better able to summarize the differing components of the project into a few short paragraphs. If a donor asks for a letter of inquiry instead of a project proposal, then you can expand your abstract to include more detail about the proposal. Usually, a letter of inquiry is approximately two pages long.

NARRATIVE PROJECT DESCRIPTION/WORK PLAN

The statement of need, sometimes referred to as a statement of the problem or needs assessment, represents the reason behind your proposal. Your statement of need specifies what conditions you specifically want to change and is where you convince the donor that the issue you want to address is appropriate to the donor's mission and important enough to merit attention and funding. This is where the NGO explains that the problem it wishes to solve is worthy of funding by the donor.

In this section, objectively describe the specific problem and community your proposal addresses. Then support your statement with research/evidence to justify the need or problem. Such research may include statistics and any other information you have gathered regarding the problem, such as personal interviews with the beneficiaries, surveys, focus groups, objective news reports, and expert commentary. By offering concrete and objective information about the situation on the ground, you set the stage for establishing the critical importance of your proposed project. Most importantly, you must clearly and persuasively prove how the problem and need(s) relate to the donor's mission and priorities. The donor must be convinced that 1) your beneficiaries are experiencing a critical need; 2) this problem can be solved; and 3) the proposal fits within the purpose of the donor's organization.

Following this problem statement, you need to explain why the issue is important. For instance, Iraqi women's lack of knowledge of the law may prevent them from pursuing legal remedies that are available to them. You would also want to explain the issue in the context you want to address it in. For example, do you want your work to encompass all of Iraq or do you want to limit it to a particular city or province/governorate? Finally, try to frame your needs statement to fit the solution your proposal suggests. For example, if the problem is that women are unaware of their rights, your solution could be to create a public awareness campaign to inform women of their rights.

Goals and Objectives

The goals and objectives of a proposal describes what the NGO plans to do about the need or problem. This section will include specific, detailed information that should convince the donor that you have a well-organized and well-thought-out program that is effective and efficient. Your goals and objectives should include the following components:

i. Goal: Goals are large statements about what you hope to accomplish. Your project can have one or more goals to solve a core issue of concern or need.

ii. Objectives: Goals are then broken down into several concrete objectives. An objective states in positive and provable terms what the project will accomplish. Each objective is further divided into one or more activities and each activity is designed to bring about a specific result that will address the identified need.

This section contains detailed information about the specific activities your organization will carry out to accomplish your objectives. In this section, you will spell out the methods or strategies through which a problem is solved.

You should emphasize your collaboration with the beneficiaries in determining which specific activities to plan and also the commitment of the beneficiaries to support and participate in these activities. Each activity should be justified by incorporating objective data such as statistics, interviews, expert commentary, or past experience. This section should also include a specific timeline and a general description of how you intend to achieve your goal and objectives.

Staffing/Administration

In this section you need to describe how many employees are needed to implement the project. An employee's qualifications for each position should be set forth, including which staff will be part-time (working only a portion of the work day), full-time (working the full work day), or volunteers. Although many people can not afford to donate their time for free, they may be willing to work for some other form of compensation, such as food or literacy education. Donors like to know what role volunteers or interns will play in your project, as they are cost-effective. Do not exaggerate or underestimate your staffing requirements—simply give a realistic estimate of how many people it will take to accomplish your goals.

Donors want to know whether a project is successful or not. Therefore, donors require a detailed plan for how you will measure your program's accomplishments and effectiveness. In order to do so, you must monitor your program's progress by comparing the steps you have completed with the levels of progress in the Activities/ Methodology section of your proposal.

As part of the evaluation, you need to identify what will be evaluated. Look to the measurable objectives you identified earlier in your plan to show you what to evaluate. To evaluate a project, identify specific indicators that will objectively measure your progress both quantitatively and qualitatively.

Make sure to determine the methods you will use to evaluate each objective and specify the information you need and how you will collect it.

Most grants require reports on your organization's progress in completing a project. Therefore, it is essential to provide the donor with periodic reports throughout the project cycle. Once the project is complete, you must evaluate the program in its entirety as most donors require a final comprehensive report.

Additionally, the donor will want to know that either: 1) the project will be complete when the grant money is finished at the end of the project period stated in the grant; or 2) the project will be self-sustaining (*e.g.*, generate revenue for its own continuation). Keep in mind that donors like to know the long-term financial viability of a project to be funded.

While writing your proposal, always remember to provide the donor with as much detail as possible; assume the donor knows nothing about your project. A detailed proposal shows the donor that you have invested a lot of time and energy into planning this project. A donor is more likely to fund a project that is well-planned and well-organized than one that is well written but not well thought out.

Budget

A budget can be defined as "an itemized summary of an organization's expected income and expenses over a specified period of time." Thus, the budget is divided in two parts: 1) income and 2) expenditures. The income section should include all project funding sources.

The expenditures section is divided between administrative costs and project costs. Administrative costs represent a percentage of the overall administrative costs of your organization that are dedicated to the specific project, including percentages of individuals' salaries and benefits as well as office supplies.

Project costs should come from your previous itemization of all resources needed for each activity you have planned. The budget should include a monetary amount for each resource. The budget should be in a chart format with accompanying notes explaining any unusual items. Different grants may have differing requirements for the budget format and/or content, so be sure to check the specific requirements for each grant!

ORGANIZATION BIOGRAPHY AND BACKGROUND INFORMATION

Providing the donor with your organization's biography demonstrates your capacity to carry out the proposed project and your credibility by demonstrating organizational experience dealing with the problem to be solved or the community to be served. An organization's biography includes a brief history of the organization that includes its mission, vision, and past programs. You will also want to describe the structure of your organization plus the expertise of your management and other personnel. Your strengths and previous successes should be emphasized, as well as any awards your organization may have received. You should also include information about your board of directors, including its size and the level of participation of its members in your organization. The organizational information should be related to the project goal to demonstrate how your expertise and experience will ensure a successful project.

BUDGETING

Budgeting is an important part of the financial management of your organization. All non-governmental organizations operate under budgeting constraints. Therefore, it is essential to focus on cost-effective strategies and clear and precise budgeting. Budgeting is an activity that will last for the duration of your project; at the earliest planning stages, establishing a general budget will ensure that the project planning remains within realistic constraints. Moreover, responsible financial management includes ensuring that actual costs do not exceed budgeted costs. After the project's completion, the budget will serve as a useful indicator and will help determine the cost-effectiveness of your project. If you were able to achieve all your objectives within the budget constraints, your project is considered cost-effective. The first step to ensuring successful budgeting is to establish a strong accounting system.

Accounting

Accounting is the act of recording and analyzing an organization's financial activities and status. Accounting will allow you to collect and organize the information necessary to create an accurate and feasible budget. Non-governmental organizations must generally disclose their financial records to the public, but the requirements and procedures vary by country, so it is important to check with your government to confirm you are fulfilling all necessary duties. An accounting report usually includes four financial categories:

1) Assets: the amount of money (cash and value of equipment) your organization has.
2) Liabilities: the amount of money your organization owes.
3) Revenue: the amount of money your organization is raising.
4) Expenses: the amount of money your organization is spending.

Whether financial records are handwritten in an

accounting journal or stored on the computer, they need to include: 1) a statement of revenues and expenses; and 2) a balance sheet.

Statement of Revenues and Expenses

The statement of revenues and expenses will consist of an itemized list of revenues and expenses the organization has received or paid in the current month and the year-to-date in the form of a spreadsheet. The last row of the spreadsheet will show the balance (revenues minus expenses). The statement of revenues and expenses allows an organization to see the money raised and money spent in a specific time period.

Balance Sheet

A balance sheet uses the same format as a statement of revenues and expenses, but it charts assets and liabilities. Examples of assets include: cash, inventories, property, land, and equipment. Examples of liabilities include: outstanding bills, staff costs, general bills, and loans. The balance sheet also includes a fund balance at the end, which is the same as the fund balance from the statement of revenues. The balance sheet differs from the statement of revenues and expenses in that it is cumulative and not limited to the financial fluctuations of the current year; it also includes the outstanding surpluses or deficits since the foundation of the organization.

After gathering the relevant financial information and organizing it through the aforementioned accounting procedures, your organization will develop an annual operating budget.

Annual Operating Budget

All NGOs must develop an annual budget. This can be difficult given that it will require you to estimate and anticipate future income and expenses. After outlining the potential income resources and estimating the amount of resources your organization will receive in the coming year, individuals or teams within your organization should develop program outlines, including general estimates of budgetary requirements. Then, the director of your organization will review these requirements with the board of directors and other organizational officers and determine an operating budget. Finally, the staff members responsible for making policy within your NGO must review the operating budget and develop programs that fulfil the mission of your organization while remaining within the budget constraints. As sources of funding are often uncertain, your budget will often need to be revised upon receipt of a new grant.

Project Budgets

In addition to an annual operating budget, each individual project requires its own budget. A detailed budget is a requirement for every grant proposal. It entails identifying each activity your program will include in the project and listing every resource required, along with a monetary value for each item. Many donors have specific requirements or formats for your budget and you will need to follow their guidelines exactly. However, regardless of the format, certain categories must be included in any budget.

The first element to a successful budget is putting each item under the correct category. When itemizing a budget, make sure every section of the budget correlates to the narrative proposal. Make the budget easy to read and understand.

Include the name of your organization, the title of the project, the time period or duration of the project, and the total budget required, including the currency you are working with. Your budget will also need to include certain categories of costs.

A budget is usually divided into two categories: direct and indirect costs. Direct costs, or project costs, are identified as those specific to the proposal and include such matters as staff (salaries and benefits), equipment, services, supplies, travel, and consultants. Indirect costs, or administrative costs, are expenses that do not attach to the specific proposal, such as office space rental, utilities, and other general administrative costs.

Each cost will need a column for description of the cost, the unit, the unit price, and the number of units required and a total for that cost. The final column is a space for notes on any items that require explanation or clarification. If you need to explain in greater detail any unusual costs, you can describe them in a budget narrative.

Although these will depend on your specific project, some examples include:

1. Facility rental for seminars/workshops;
2. Program Staff;
3. Food and Refreshments;
4. Pamphlets or Informational Materials; and
5. Required Equipment.

Some costs, such as office equipment, including computers and printers, are fixed costs and do not need to be included in the project budget.

The final element of a project budget is a contingency category, normally 5%, which is specified for any unforeseen expenses that may arise during the course of the project cycle. (The sample project budget provided at the end of this section shows where the 5% contingency should be placed in a budget). Donors differ on their policy regarding the contingency category and administrative costs. Some may not allow for any money to be budgeted in either category and others may limit the administrative costs to a percentage of your project costs. The guidelines listed here are merely a general overview of potential categories. You must obtain and strictly follow the specific guidelines of your donor.

NGO CAPACITY-BUILDING REFERENCE MANUAL

This reference guide will enable non-governmental organizations (NGOs) in Iraq to gain a general understanding of how an NGO is defined. It also summarizes the types of NGOs based on organizational structures and the kinds of services they provide. Over the years, NGOs have become key instruments of change on the community, national, and international levels. As there are many different types of NGOs and other actors in civil society, it is critical to define what constitutes an NGO in order to differentiate it from other organizations.

The term "non-governmental organization" was adopted by the United Nations when it agreed to provide a mechanism for citizen-based participation in the United Nations. As NGOs evolved over the years, definitions of what constitutes an NGO have become more diverse. They now encompass a wide-range of organizations—from international to community-based organizations—that provide a wide variety of services. However, most agree that all NGOs have several defining characteristics that differentiate them from other types of associations. For instance, the World Bank defines NGOs as "private organizations that pursue activities to relieve suffering, promote the interests of the poor, protect the environment, provide basic social services or undertake community development." Others define NGOs as "groups or institutions that are entirely or largely independent of the government and that have primarily humanitarian or cooperative rather than commercial objectives." In sum, the term NGO refers to a non-profit (i.e., an organization that does not make a profit) organization that operates independently from the government and addresses issues in support of the public good.

Certain fundamental characteristics differentiate NGOs from political interest groups or commercial organizations. These characteristics are as follows:

- Non-profit: NGOs are run as not-for-profit enterprises. They primarily have humanitarian or cooperative rather than commercial objectives.
- Independent from government control: Although some NGOs may accept government funding for certain projects and activities, their operation is not controlled by the government.
- Do not constitute a political party: While some NGOs may be affiliated with a political party, an NGO does not seek to challenge a government as a political party.
- Non-violent: NGOs must have a commitment to non-violence and must not engage in violent methods to achieve their goals.
- Voluntary membership: NGOs are comprised of members who join on a voluntary basis and who are driven by a common interest. Working for the public good and volunteerism is generally associated with NGOs.

- Common purpose/mission: NGOs are created to perform a variety of service and humanitarian functions, as defined by their mission.

The above-mentioned characteristics of NGOs are not always entirely applicable. For instance, NGOs can be closely identified with a political party. International NGOs ("INGOs") such as the Red Cross, an international relief agency, receive money from governments for humanitarian operations. However, NGOs never constitute political parties, corporations, businesses, or insurgent groups.

CATEGORIES OF NGOS

The term "NGO" covers a wide range of organizations. Generally, NGOs "perform a variety of services and humanitarian functions, bring citizens' concerns to governments, advocate and monitor policies, and encourage political participation through provision of information." They range from international organizations such as the Red Cross to local, community-based groups found in developing countries. NGOs also include professional associations, grassroots organizations, and research institutes.

NGOs are generally categorized as either: (i) operational NGOs, whose primary purpose is to implement development programs; or (ii) advocacy NGOs, whose primary purpose is to seek and defend a particular cause and advocate for change in the political system, whether at the regional, national, or international level. Despite their different purposes, both operational and advocacy NGOs engage in many of the same activities, including fundraising, mobilizing volunteers, organizing special events, and using the media to achieve their goals.

Although both categories are generally referred to as NGOs, some organizations make the distinction between NGOs and civil society organizations (CSOs). When the distinction is made between the two, NGO refers to operational NGOs and CSOs refer to both operational and advocacy NGOs. The World Bank and the United Nations further classify operational NGOs into three groups: (i) community-based organizations (CBOs), which deal with issues limited to a local region; (ii) national organizations; and (iii) international organizations, which are headquartered in one country but carry out development projects in more than one country.

CBOs (sometimes referred to as "grassroots" organizations) are usually comprised of members who join to further their own mutual interest, such as youth groups, women's associations, and credit circles. They are more likely to receive project goods and services, whereas national and international NGOs usually provide services, design projects, or give technical assistance. Although global statistics on the number of NGOs are incomplete, it is generally believed that hundreds of thousands of CBOs exist throughout the world.

Whether an NGO is organized to provide development services, such as credit for poor women or to advocate for change, local, national, and international organizations play an essential role in providing services and ideas that are often not provided by governments. This is especially true in countries where people are frustrated by corrupt governments or inefficient economies.

NGO STRENGTHS AND WEAKNESSES

Since NGOs vary according to their expertise, mandate, size of membership, resources, mission, activities, and the overall quality of their work, it is difficult to make generalizations as to the strengths and weaknesses of NGOs. However, the World Bank, which has years of global development experience, has compiled such a list. This broad list of strengths and weaknesses of the NGO system is a useful starting point for identifying key areas where capacity-building is needed to ensure the sustainability of NGOs.

The World Bank lists the following strengths:

- Strong grassroots links;
- Field-based development expertise;
- The ability to adapt and innovate;
- Participatory methodologies and tools;
- Long-term commitment; and
- Cost-effectiveness.

The World Bank identifies NGO weaknesses as:

- Limited financial and management expertise;
- Limited institutional capacity;
- Low-level of sustainability;
- Isolation and lack of inter-organizational communication;
- Small-scale interventions; and
- Lack of understanding of the broader, social, and economic context.

Many of the weaknesses listed above, however, can be mitigated through training, technical advice, and proper management of NGOs. Furthermore, local NGOs can minimize their isolation through the use of technologies and low communication costs to form coalitions with other like-minded organizations.

All NGOs, regardless of size, mandate, or geographical location, serve a critical role in both international and national civil society. Some NGOs work in the international arena to advocate for change at the United Nations and the World Bank as well as monitor international agreements. Other international NGOs provide humanitarian relief to victims of major disasters, while community-based NGOs provide local services such as job-training and literacy classes for women in their villages. All NGOs, however, strive to play an active role in effecting societal change for the better.

8

Recommendations of the NGO Platform

On 26-27 September 2006, about 80 European NGO representatives, active against trafficking in human beings, came together at the second La Strada International NGO Platform in Kiev, Ukraine. During these two days, the NGO representatives, among which the nine La Strada member organisations, shared their thoughts and experiences, in particular with regard to their own role in the anti-trafficking field as watchdogs and service providers. Discussions were linked to the overall theme of the NGO platform 2006: 'anti-trafficking activity towards safe migration perspectives'. This theme was specifically chosen in support of the UN Year of Migration. The following recommendations are based on the outcome of discussions and recommendations made in the various working group sessions.

The NGOs present stressed the need for civil society and NGOs in Europe to be represented and respected as important actors in the anti-trafficking field. NGOs contribute significantly to the fight against trafficking in human beings through their advocacy and information work, their prevention programmes and, in particular, their direct assistance to trafficked persons. Local, national and European governments should therefore take their consultation and advice into account and actively involve NGOs when developing national and European action plans, policies and infrastructure to address the issue.

Next to Action Plans, NGOs call for the effective implementation of National Referral Mechanisms (NRM). Because NGOs are still the main service providers to trafficked persons and are responsible for national as well as local information and assistance hotlines on the issue of trafficking in human beings, they should play an essential role in National Referral Mechanisms. A National Referral Mechanism (NRM) is a cooperative framework through which state actors fulfil their obligations to protect and promote the human rights of trafficked persons, coordinating their efforts in a strategic partnership with civil society. The NGOs that were present believe that in their lobby on NRMs towards governments, they themselves should take into account that:

- Advocacy efforts to support the implementation of a National Referral Mechanism should be based on specific and clear messages that are aimed at the responsible institutes and persons. Messages should be developed and delivered jointly together with other relevant stakeholders such as non-governmental organisations, national rapporteurs, ombudspersons and donors agencies.
- Transnational exchange of experience and cooperation should be used to inform about NGO advocacy efforts by highlighting good practice models abroad as well as by monitoring case studies in countries of destination, transit and origin.

- National action plans should be used as a tool for monitoring the implementation of various components of the National Referral Mechanism.
- The operational and policy aspects of NGO work should be linked by building advocacy arguments and messages informed by both, grassroots service provision work and international standards.
- Within the NRM, activities are monitored and evaluated in order to propose reforms. NGOs should use training as a measure to build relations with key partners within the NRM and to change attitudes so that later different stakeholders will be more receptive to advocacy messages and recommendations for reform of the NRM.

They call upon other NGOs active in the fight against trafficking in human beings, to take the above into account as well. It is felt that a clear distinction between the role of NGOs and the role of governments should be made. Next to close cooperation with governments, NGOs see their role as monitors (watchdogs) for governmental actions, in particular to ensure that when governments implement their actions, the human rights of trafficked persons are respected. Although the term 'human rights' is very popular these days and frequently used by all actors, the proposed actions, policies and measures are often not based on the essential human rights principles or they do not protect the human rights of the affected groups. In the international anti-trafficking debate, too much focus is still put on repressive strategies to fight trafficking, instead on empowering strategies to prevent trafficking.

NGOs therefore call for the implementation of a human rights based approach in anti-trafficking activity.

Governments should implement non-harmful anti-trafficking strategies and address harmful policies and actions. In addition, monitoring and evaluation mechanisms should be established to evaluate actions. NGOs are aware that also their own actions and organisations should be monitored and evaluated to make sure that their actions are not counterproductive or even negatively affect the rights and position of trafficked persons. To avoid this, they are committed:

- To make more conscious use of human rights based principles in the practice of their organisations/structure, as well as in the decision making process.
- To continue the discussion on a human rights based approach in anti-trafficking initiatives, but also in the way this approach is applied at the NGO organisational level.
- To strengthen and encourage a participatory approach also on advocacy and lobbying level.
- To create a check list of human rights principles that NGOs can use to monitor their programmes and to evaluate how well the principles of a human rights based approach are followed.

The present NGOs call upon other NGOs active in the anti-trafficking field to commit to the above principles as well. Next to the protection of human rights, the present NGOs also urge governments to address prevention of trafficking further and to focus more on root causes of trafficking in the countries of origin and destination, such as poverty, unequal gender relations, traditional social structures, the lack of safe and legal migration possibilities and the demand for cheap and exploited (irregular) labour.

The issue of trafficking should be looked at from a broader perspective, including other forms of labour exploitation and the human right to migrate. The trafficking debate so far has concentrated too much on trafficking for sexual exploitation and sought solutions in specific prostitution policies. The aspect of safe migration possibilities and labour rights for migrant workers-in order to prevent trafficking-has hardly been explored. The NGO platform therefore urges governments to sign and ratify the International Convention on the Protection of the Rights of All Migrant Workers and Members of Their Families. It also calls for guarantees to safe migration and migrant protection, referring to the guidelines that PICUM developed to protect migrant workers.

In order to address this issue further, NGOs active against trafficking in human beings should:

- Develop closer ties with migrant rights organisations.
- Work towards reliable data collection and 'proof' collection; the NGO Platform should be used to set up a data exchange/collection forum.
- Better use the legal system to claim human rights. If there are no anti-trafficking laws, make better use of labour and human right legislation, for example, the claim for compensation to be granted to trafficked persons.
- Strengthen advocacy efforts, using public shame, ethical branding, fair trade and other methods to advocate for access to social systems and for obtaining a legal status for undocumented migrants.

NGOs have noticed that the trafficking debate has become highly politicised and polarised. For NGOs, the main goal is the protection of the rights of trafficked persons and affected groups as well as their empowerment. NGOs therefore protest against States and donors who want to impose their political and ideological ideas on NGOs through financial pressure and are concerned about the political, social and cultural pressures NGOs face in countries of origin and destination. NGOs call for financial support from governments and donor agencies for their work, but believe that NGOs should at all times remain independent from and critical towards governments and donors, regarding existing actions, policies and criteria. In order to improve funding possibilities for anti-trafficking activity, anti-trafficking NGOs should:

- Jointly lobby towards donors for funding for NGOs, in particular for anti-trafficking work.
- Support and cooperate each other in fundraising efforts, but remain critical to partners they cooperate with and the project proposals that are made.
- Establish donor criteria and be critical towards donors and other sources of financing. NGOs should be cautious not to become too dependent on donors and not to automatically accept all criteria donors put on them. NGOs should use negotiations to get funding for the activities they want to implement.
- Try to reach sustainability and try to receive different forms of income.
- Fulfil certain standards, e.g. being a reliable partner for donors and other NGOs.

NGOs further call for structural actions and the minimisation of ad hoc initiatives, set up arbitrarily after public and political debates, such as the actions around the World Football Cup in Germany. The present NGOs believe these actions are less effective and might do more harm than good. Regarding hotlines, anti-trafficking NGOs believe that:

- Hotlines on trafficking issues should be independent, confidential and not temporary, as hotlines need time to develop and become effective.
- Hotlines should be promoted with a strong campaign using various forms of publicity.
- Hotlines should be part of a National Referral Mechanism.
- New problems or developments in the field of trafficking should be linked to existing hotlines.
- Hotline consultation should be linked with other new methods of consultation (e-mail, online counselling), which should be investigated and further developed.
- There is an urgent need for training hotline managers and consultants.

With regard to prevention programmes, NGOs should cooperate closely with other actors. When establishing prevention programmes NGOs should keep in mind that:

- Materials for training and prevention work should be based on reliable research and respond to trends identified through research and service provision.
- Prevention work should ideally be developed and implemented with a participatory approach. The target audience should be actively involved in the design and activities. This way prevention work is not only about information, but also about empowerment and supporting others to be proactive.

- Prevention activities should be regularly monitored and feedback should be requested from target audiences so that materials and methods can be adapted in the future to be more effective.
- Prevention programmes should also ensure motivation and further training for specialists and trainers. For example, this can be done through participation in international meetings and through facilitated exchange of experiences and good practice.
- Different methods should be developed to reach different audiences. We should consider how best to use media and new technologies in our prevention work.

THE GLOBAL COMPACT AND HUMAN RIGHTS

The Global Compact Office would like to thank the team at Wilton Park and the UK Foreign & Commonwealth Office for putting together this promising conference. Sphere of influence and complicity-core themes at this conference-are key concepts for the Global Compact. "Sphere of influence" is actually a phrase that the Global Compact introduced to the field of corporate citizenship/ CSR, and "complicity" is a concept that the Compact has helped to popularize in this context. We welcome the opportunity to discuss the concepts in detail and hope for viable suggestions for how to give them practical meaning for companies and other organizations around the world. We are delighted to be associated with, and to have contributed to the preparations for, this event. We hope to pick up some new ideas to make our own business and human rights work programme more effective.

As important background for this event, we would like to offer the following refresher on the Global Compact, our approach to human rights and the role of the Compact in the context of calls for greater accountability for business.

REFRESHER ON THE GLOBAL COMPACT

The Global Compact was introduced in 1999 because many felt that globalization was not delivering all it had promised. In particular, its benefits were dramatically unevenly distributed. Although the primary responsibility for implementing international agreements on human rights, labour standards, the environment and anti-corruption lies with governments, business was seen as having an important role to play.

In fact, one of the founding premises of the GC is that without active involvement of business, there is the danger that universal principles, including those embodied in international human rights instruments, will remain unimplemented. The Global Compact emphasizes the business case for improved social and environmental performance and business' own operations and activities not the traditional CSR concept that is based on philanthropy. We believe that the largest impact that business can have is through conducting their business in a sustainable way that respects human rights and limits their environmental impact, treats their workers well and avoids corruption.

The Compact, itself, is both a set of universal principles and a network-based multi-stakeholder initiative with a change model for how to raise the level of business' social and environment performance. The Secretary-General derived the principles from international instruments that enjoy wide consensus like the UDHR, ILO Declaration, Rio Declaration, and UN Convention Against Corruption. Businesses initiate their participation through a commitment by their CEO endorsed by their Board expressing their support for the principles and their intention to work towards their implementation within their own operations.

This is a key element of the Compact's leadership model. Effective positive change requires a leadership commitment and it is our intention that change agents inside companies will use their CEO's expression of commitment to help them to more easily make necessary changes inside the company to improve its social and environmental performance.

The Global Compact is not a seal of approval for or endorsement of the companies or other organizations participating in it. Nor is it a regulatory or compliance based model. The Global Compact Office has neither the mandate nor the resources for that.

As a result, we encourage improved performance and positive change through the means available to us as an initiative inside the UN Secretariat: learning, dialogue, networks, initiatives, projects and promoting greater transparency around company social and environmental efforts. We also work with the financial incentive system within which companies operate to encourage the mainstream financial community to take into account companies' social and environmental performance in making their valuations. Global Compact Office was established in July 2000 with less than 50 companies. Today, there are 2268 participating companies in 87 countries, dozens of civil society and labour organizations and more than 40 local networks engaged.

THE GLOBAL COMPACT'S APPROACH TO HUMAN RIGHTS

Two of the Global Compact's ten principles are devoted to human rights. However, the labour standards principles are also human rights related. The two human rights principles are positive and negative, that is, they emphasize doing good as well as not doing harm. Human rights is a major priority area of the UN Global Compact Office as it remains one of the newest and least familiar for many of the company participants. We've been doing a fair bit of work in this area and plan to continue doing so. We feel we are making an important contribution although much more clearly remains to be done.

Our main partner in all our human rights work has been and will remain the OHCHR. They are clearly the guardians of the two human rights principles. We also work with a number of other organizations in this area, including BLIHR and the Danish Institute for Human Rights. Located within the UN Secretariat-the Secretary-General's office to be precise-the Global Compact Office must be as pragmatic and non political as possible. We focus on the practical "How" question, namely, how to implement human rights within a business's own operations and activities, especially on what businesses can do to eliminate their potentially negative human rights impact. Two recent publications that we have produced in this area are: Raising the Bar; and Embedding HR in Business Practice. One of our major activities in this area has been fostering tool development and recommending proven tools to help with the implementation process. Rather than reinvent the wheel, we help disseminate information about existing tools with a proven track record, such as the Business & Human

Rights Resource Centre's website, the Danish Institute Human Rights Compliance Assessment quick check tool, and the BLIHR matrix. We are also working on a human rights training package and, with partners, on a business guide to human rights impact assessment and, with BLIHR, on guidance for managers on how to implement human rights.

One of our most significant contributions to the area continues to be our efforts to build consensus among companies, other societal actors and even governments that human rights are an important business issue. Our leadership model is key here. The process for initiating involvement (CEO commitment with endorsement from the Board) means that many boardroom and/or senior executive discussions about human rights have taken place because of the Global Compact. Moreover, 2268 companies are on record as having expressed support for and intention to implement human rights. Importantly, these are companies in 87 different countries, helping to demonstrate the universality of human rights. Governments have also collectively and individually recognized the contribution of the Global Compact in a number of contexts, most recently in the 2005 World Summit Outcome document.

We are pleased to report that much learning is going on at the local level. We know that some Global Compact local networks have used our human rights publication as the basis for running their own learning activities on human rights. Many Global Compact local networks have also invited local chapters of human rights NGOs to come and speak with them to help them learn about human rights in a business context. In some countries where governments are not very supportive of human rights, business has been taking a keen interest and are slowly helping their governments to see that human rights are important.

We have also contributed to the business and human rights debate through helping to develop and refine its lexicon. As already mentioned, we helped popularize the concepts of "sphere of influence" and "complicity" as key terms that have helped focus and advance the business and human rights debate. We also collect and disseminate case studies of the real dilemmas that companies are facing and provide opportunities for companies and others to come together to work on solutions. E.g. Supply chain, business in conflict zones (Enabling economies of peace), managing diversity and non-discrimination, and contributing to OHCHR's consultation process last year. As the UN, we can bring to the table audiences that others sometimes can't.

Is our approach having an impact? McKinsey & Company's impact assessment in 2004 found that the Compact has existential power and has had significant incremental impact in the sense of helping change to happen faster and more easily-which is our modest aim. Among the other findings were that half of all participating companies reported having changed their policies with respect to the principles. Many companies from OECD countries have signed on to Global Compact to learn about how to improve their human rights performance. For nearly two-thirds of the companies from developing countries, the Global Compact is the first corporate citizenship initiative in which they have engaged. Many do so to learn how to improve their social and environmental performance and thus enhance their ability to enter into supplier relationships with larger global firms. There is no doubt that much more remains to be done. One of our most exciting upcoming challenges is that we're bringing our multi-stakeholder approach to China with a big Summit there later this year.

GREATER LEGAL ACCOUNTABILITY FOR BUSINESS

A word or two is also warranted on the role of the Global Compact in the context of calls for greater legal accountability for business. The first point to note is that the Global Compact is a voluntary initiative without a mandate or resources to monitor compliance. Nevertheless, protecting the integrity of the UN and of the initiative is a legitimate concern. We therefore introduced a stricter logo protection policy and new integrity measures covering misuse of the GC logo and a complaint procedure for systematic and egregious abuse of the GC's overall aim and principles. The policy goes as far as UN legal office will allow given our status as voluntary initiative of UN Secretariat.

We also introduced a procedural requirement that all company participants communicate to their stakeholders on a regular basis their progress in implementing all ten principles. Companies not doing so for two years in a row are designated "inactive" on our website until they start communicating.

This has already started to show results with media calling attention to "inactive" companies, prompting them to start communicating. Most importantly of all, we cannot emphasize enough that the Global Compact's voluntary initiative is not intended to be a total solution.

It is positioned as complementary to and not a substitute for other approaches, including for international law. Human rights issues are complex and a multitude of approaches is clearly needed. The Global Compact is an important tool in the quest to advance the business and human rights agenda. Too often the business and human rights debate is presented as if there is a dichotomy between voluntary and regulatory approaches as if it is either/or. This is a false dichotomy. There is a huge demand for consensus building, tools and practical solution finding. The Global Compact is a key platform that can help in this regard and thereby contribute to better implementation of human rights.

THE INTERNET AND HUMAN RIGHTS: AN OVERVIEW

The Internet is a unique communications medium. Like no other medium before, it allows individuals to express their ideas and opinions directly to a world audience and easily to each other, while allowing access to many more ideas, opinions and information than previous media have allowed. Consequently, there is a vital connection between the Internet and human rights.

Threatened by Governmental Restrictions

Through the Internet, citizens from the most repressive regimes are able to find information about matters concerning their own governments and their human rights records that no newspaper may dare print, while denouncing the conditions under which they live, for the world to hear. The Internet allows an intimate look at other countries, other people and other cultures that few before were ever able to attain. This power to give and receive information, so central to any conception of democracy, can be truly achieved on the Internet, as nowhere before.

Further, through the use of encryption technology, citizens can have instantaneous communications with individuals all over the world that are much more resistant to government and private surveillance. On the Internet, citizens are not mere consumers of content but also creators of content. This fundamental shift in power has created a possibility for every individual to be a publisher. Consequently, the content on the Internet is as diverse as human thought. Individuals and communities have been using the new-found freedom online to link, interact and work collectively in this global work space. The effect of access to and use of this global interactive medium has been to promote and defend civil and political rights worldwide. This unprecedented power, however, can be very threatening to repressive regimes. The experiences of communities in different countries indicates that few things could be more threatening to authoritarian regimes than access and use of a medium that knows no boundaries and is very hard to control. While traditional methods of censorship-embargoing newspapers and closing down presses-do not work on the Internet, the online censoring techniques that these regimes attempt can be just as destructive.

While the Internet is technologically resistant to government control, it is not immune from such control. Indeed, some countries have been quite sophisticated in exploiting the control and surveillance potential to great effect, at least in the short run. Just because the younger generation may know how to "hack" through proxy servers to avoid censorship does not mean that the youth are safe. These actions should be understood in the technological context--that such hacking is probably obvious to government system administrators, and may make people vulnerable to being identified and prosecuted. Meanwhile, nations around the world are seeking to exploit the surveillance potential of this new medium, including by asserting control over the design and development of communications networks to maximize their surveillance capabilities.

For these reasons, governments and regional and international bodies should enact enforceable free expression guarantees, promote widespread access to and use of strong cryptographic tools that will enable real security, and provide legal protections of privacy, including controls on government surveillance.

The Internet and Human Rights Work

The Internet is one of the best means for communicating on human rights, because it is inexpensive and global. E-mail makes point-to-point communication between human rights workers and among NGOs (non-governmental organizations) cheap and easy, and allows for better coordination of actions.

Furthermore, the Internet has the potential of reaching global audiences, including those most in need of such information. The Internet is important to those working for human rights, as it can provide a secure means of communicating between and coordinating the work of human rights groups. Consequently, human rights activists were among the first to make use of the Internet to--

- Coordinate actions and make contacts. Perhaps the most important application of the Internet in human rights is as a great tool for NGOs and activists to be in touch with each other, to share information privately, and to coordinate actions.
- Expose human rights violations and let people know about them. Many human rights organizations throughout the world have instituted e-mail lists

to propagate their press releases, alerts and denunciations vis a vis human rights violations. Many of these groups also use Usenet to post their information, or it is posted there by others, and many groups have instituted web pages to make information available.

- Solicit action. Many organizations now use e-mail to distribute action alerts calling for letters to be written on behalf of specific issues.
- Gather information. The amount of human rights information online is extraordinary-beginning with the University of Minnesota web site, and now with the UNHCHR (United Nations High Commissioner on Human Rights) site online, it's much easier to do human rights research.

By enabling early access to information, immediate dissemination of calls for campaigns, and the organization of wide international pressure, the Internet greatly increases the lobbying capacities of human rights groups. It is vitally important, therefore, to promote freedom of expression and privacy as central elements of the development of the information society.

Internet Freedom in the US

Unfortunately, the US government's domestic policy has not been fully supportive of human rights on the Internet. The US Congress has twice enacted censorship legislation attempting to control content on the Internet.

Under our strong constitutional protection of free speech, these laws have been ruled unconstitutional by the courts. Yet Members of Congress continue to press other restrictive measures, and proposals are pending to make Internet Service Providers (ISPs) liable for removing allegedly illegal or improper content. On the privacy side, the Communications Assistance for Law Enforcement Act of 1994 (CALEA) requires that telecommunications systems be designed to accommodate government surveillance, and that law has been perverted by the Department of Justice and the Federal Communications Commission to not merely preserve but to enhance government wiretap capabilities.

Only recently has the US government begun to turn away from its efforts to control the spread of encryption, which is crucial to security and privacy on the Internet. Still, officials in the Justice Department are trying to preserve their access to decryption keys, and the surveillance debate in the US is not over. Meanwhile, the US government refuses to publicly discuss its international eavesdropping activities, amid growing domestic and international concern over the nature of surveillance in a digital world and, in particular, the US government's "Echelon" surveillance system.

Internet Access Is Important to the Promotion of Human Rights

The most often disregarded impediment to the achievement of the Internet's democratic potential is the problem of access. Accessing the Internet requires either the possession of a computer and payment to an Internet Service Provider or access to a facility where one can connect. This means that, generally, only the affluent will have access.

Governments can control freedom of expression of sections of the population by hindering their access to the Internet. This may be done directly by imposing high taxes on computer products and supporting telephone monopolies that keep phone rates high and thus discourage the use of the Internet, or indirectly by failing to support community centres where people may have low-cost access to the Internet. However, augmented Net access without civil liberties guarantees ? in technology and in law ? may not benefit individuals and may be coupled with government control and extended surveillance capability.

Freedom of Expression

The Universal Declaration, the European Convention and other international human rights agreements enshrine the rights to freedom of expression and access to information. These core documents explicitly protect freedom of expression "regardless of frontiers," a phrase especially pertinent to the global Internet: "Everyone has the right to freedom of opinion and expression; this right includes freedom to hold opinions without interference and to seek, receive and impart information and ideas through any media, and regardless of frontiers." Article 19, Universal Declaration of Human Rights.

"Everyone shall have the right to freedom of expression; this right shall include freedom to seek, receive, and impart information and ideas of all kinds, regardless of frontiers, either orally, in writing or in print, in the form of art, or through any other media of his choice." Article 19, International Covenant on Civil and Political Rights. "Everyone has the right to freedom of expression.

This right shall include freedom to hold opinions and to receive and impart information and ideas without interference by public authority and regardless of borders." Article 10, European Convention for the Protection of Human Rights and Fundamental Freedoms. No matter what the means, government restrictions on speech or access to speech of others violate basic freedom of expression protections. In addition to direct government censorship of Internet communications, or privatized censorship, freedom of speech in the Internet is threatened by diverse factors.

Blocking, filtering, and labelling techniques can restrict freedom of expression and limit access to information. Government-mandated use of blocking, filtering, and label systems violates basic international human rights protections.

Global rating or labelling systems squelch the free flow of information. Efforts to force all Internet speech to be labelled or rated according to a single classification system distort the fundamental cultural diversity of the Internet and will lead to domination of one set of political or moral viewpoints.

Diversity and user choice are essential: To the extent that individuals choose to employ filtering tools, it is vital that they have access to a wide variety of such tools.

"Self-regulatory" controls over Internet content, which have been promoted by some as an alternative to government regulation, ought not to place private ISPs in the role of police officers for the Internet. With regards to content, what is being suggested in the name of "self-regulation" is not that ISPs should as a group regulate their own behaviour, but rather that they should regulate the speech of their customers. This is not true "self-regulation."

The role of an Internet Service Provider is crucial for access to the Internet and because of the crucial role that they play, ISPs have been targeted by law enforcement agencies in many countries to act as content censors. While ISPs ought to provide law enforcement reasonable assistance in investigating criminal activity, confusing the role of private companies and police authorities risks substantial violation of individual civil liberties.

Privacy

The Universal Declaration, the European Convention and international human rights instruments enshrine the right to privacy. These core documents explicitly protect the privacy of correspondence and communication: "No one shall be subjected to arbitrary interference with his privacy, family, home or correspondence, nor to attacks upon his honour and reputation. Everyone has the right to the protection of the law against such interference or attacks." Article 12, Universal Declaration of Human Rights. "No one shall be subjected to arbitrary or unlawful interference with his privacy, family, home or correspondence, nor to unlawful attacks on his honour and reputation." Article 17, International Covenant on Civil and Political Rights. "Everyone has the right to respect for his private and family life, his home and his correspondence." Article 8, European Convention for the Protection of Human Rights and Fundamental Freedoms.

Privacy is becoming increasingly important for citizens in the information society. Electronic communications can be very easily intercepted by anyone who wants to. Sending an e-mail message is thus the equivalent of sending a postcard. In the human rights arena especially, many matters discussed among NGOs are extremely confidential. Names of witnesses to human rights violations, for example, need to be kept from those who would harm them. Repressive governments commonly use their intelligence services to tap the phone communications of human rights groups and intercept their mail. It is very likely that they are also intercepting electronic mail.

How Privacy can be Protected on the Internet

Unlike phone calls and paper mail, however, electronic mail can be easily encrypted so that only those to whom it is directed can read it. This means that anyone, such as NGOs, wanting to communicate delicate information freely can do so, without having to fear the consequences of others, such as governments, accessing it. Therefore, we believe that policies concerning cryptography should be based on the fundamental right to engage in private communication.

Unfortunately, national governments have already taken steps to detain and harass users and developers of cryptography. Nonetheless, strong cryptography is already in use by human rights advocates and its further widespread use should be affirmatively promoted. We oppose efforts that would lead to the development of communications infrastructures designed for surveillance.

Anonymity

Central to free expression and the protection of privacy is the right to express political beliefs without fear of retribution and to control the disclosure of personal identity. Protecting the right of anonymity is therefore an essential goal for the protection of personal freedoms in the online world.

The right of anonymity is recognized in law and accepted by custom. It has been an integral part of the growth and development of the Internet. Some governments are working to extend techniques for anonymity. But other efforts are underway to establish mandatory identification requirements and to limit the use of techniques that protect anonymity. For example, the G-8 recently considered a proposal to require caller identification for Internet users. Some local governments have also tried to adopt legislation that would prohibit access to the Internet without the disclosure of personal identity.

Governments should not require the identification of Internet users or restrict the ability to express political beliefs on the Internet anonymously. Efforts to develop new techniques to protect anonymity and identity should be encouraged. ISPs should not establish unnecessary identification requirements for customers and should, wherever practicable, preserve the right of users to access the Internet anonymously.

9

Legitimacy, Accountability and Representation of NGOs

The first set of issues—and by far the most contentious— concerns legitimacy and accountability; who speaks for whom in an NGO alliance or network, and how are differences resolved when participants vary in strength and resources? Who enjoys the benefits and suffers the costs of what the movement achieves, especially at the grassroots level? Whose voice is heard, and which interests are ignored, when differences are filtered out in order to communicate a simple message in a global campaign? In particular, how are grassroots voices mediated by institutions of different kinds—networks and their members, northern NGOs and southern NGOs, southern NGOs and community groups, and so on down the line ?

In the mid-1990s, North American NGOs claimed to represent a southern consensus against the replenishment of the International Development Association (IDA), the soft loan arm of the World Bank, on the grounds that social and environmental safeguards were too weak. In contrast, southern NGOs (mainly from Africa) insisted that the IDA go ahead regardless of the weakness of these safeguards, because foreign aid was desperately needed even if its terms were imperfect. The "banana wars" of 1998-99 provide a more recent example of this problem, where NGOs supporting small-scale banana producers in Central America and the Caribbean found themselves on opposite sides of a landmark dispute before the World Trade Organization.

On some issues (like debt or landmines), there is a solid south-north consensus in favour of a unified lobbying position. However, in other areas (especially trade and labour rights and the environment), there is no such consensus, since people and their civic representatives may have conflicting short-term interests in different parts of the world. As globalization proceeds, these areas will become the centrepiece of the international system's response, so it is vital that NGO networks develop a more sophisticated way of addressing differences of opinion within civil society in different localities and regions. Very few networks have mechanisms in place of resolve such differences democratically.

In cases like these, discussions often focus on the thorny issue of representation, though there are really two questions that are being asked: first, is representation the only route to NGO legitimacy in global governance? Second, how "representative" must an organization be in order to qualify for a seat at the negotiating table? These questions are often conflated, with results that make sensible discussion of policy options impossible.

Legitimacy is generally understood as the right to be and do something in society, a sense that an organization is lawful, admissible, and justified in its chosen course of action; but there are different ways in which these things can be validated. Legitimacy in membership bodies is claimed through the normal democratic processes of election and formal sanctions that ensure that an agency is representative of, and accountable to, its constituents. Trade unions and some NGO federations fall into this category, though whether these processes operate effectively and democratically is another matter. Agreeing on some minimum standards in this regard is an important part of the agenda for the future. A small number of intermediary NGOs also have a membership base of this kind (Amnesty International is a good example), but most do not, and very few international NGO networks have democratic systems of governance of accountability. This creates obvious problems in claiming legitimacy through representation; these problems are exacerbated by the financial gains that come from serving as a trusted intermediary for donors who want to fund NGO advocacy, but who cannot make grants directly to every participant. This sets up an unhealthy dynamic, since NGOs in Washington, London, or Brussels have a vested interest in maintaining the role of intermediary rather than encouraging NGOs, especially those based in the south, to represent themselves directly. The financial implications of losing this precious status are one reason why criticisms of legitimacy touch off such a fierce reaction among northern NGOs; this is one of the rawest of NGO nerves.

In their defence, intermediary NGOs do not need democratic ways of sustaining their legitimacy, since their legitimacy is defined by legal compliance, effective supervision by their trustees, and recognition by other legitimate bodies that they have valuable knowledge and skills to bring to the debate. Since global governance is inevitably going to be a combination of formal and informal political processes, it is perfectly possible for NGOs to be legitimate but not representative participants in global debates, so long as they are clear on the implications of the different ways in which legitimacy is claimed. No one expects Oxfam, for example, to be perfectly representative of developing world opinion; only that its proposals on debt and other issues should be solidly rooted in research and experience and sensitive to the views and aspirations of its developing world partners. However, even if Oxfam conforms to these conditions (which is a challenge in itself), this gives them no formal rights to participate in global decision-making, since this is an area in which legitimacy must be claimed through representation. Non-membership bodies may have the right to a voice, but not to a vote. In this sense, the best representative of civil society is a democratically elected government, complemented by the checks and balances provided by non-state membership bodies (such as labour unions) and pressure groups of different kinds. The resulting mix will be very messy, but it is standard practice in national politics and looks set to shape the emergence of more democratic regimes at the global level too. The world will never be perfectly democratic, but it can be increasingly pluralist, and if that pluralism allows all interests to be represented and debated then a better set of decisions will emerge over time.

It is no accident that questions about legitimacy are being raised at a time when NGOs have started to gain real influence on the international stage. In that sense they are victims of their own success. Neither is there any shortage of hypocrisy among the critics, especially when it appears that NGOs are being singled out in contrast to businesses (and even many governments) that are even less accountable than they are. Nevertheless, the criticism are real, and must be addressed if NGOs are to exploit the political space that has opened up in the post-Cold War world. At minimum, that means no more unsubstantiated claims to "represent the people" and more concerted and creative efforts to change the balance of power in global civil alliances. This will always be difficult but, when different routes to legitimacy are confused, the issues are impossible to resolve in any sensible way.

NGOs: From The Local to the Global

Globalization requires both governments and NGOs to link different levels of their activity together—local, notional, regional, and global. For governments this challenge is somewhat more straightforward, since they have a chain of intergovernmental structures like the United Nations through which debate and decision-making can be linked, at least in theory. The situation is much more challenging for NGOs, since there are no parallel structures to facilitate supernational civic participation, and no civic representation in intergovernmental bodies.

All around the world, governments, NGOs, and businesses are already experimenting with "dialogic politics" at the local level, sharing in planning and decision-making to generate a better and more sustainable set of outcomes. These experiments are the local building blocks of future global governance. By laying a strong foundation for negotiations over labour standards, environmental pollution, and human rights, they offer the potential to connect ordinary citizens to global regimes. But this can only work if local structures are connected to more democratic structures at higher levels of the world system, helping to ensure that sacrifices made in one locality are not exploited by less scrupulous parties elsewhere. Recent tripartite agreements on child labour in Bangladeshi garment factories are a sign of the future in this respect, with NGOs, government, and business striking mutually advantageous local begains within a framework of global minimum standards set out in the provisions of International Labour Organization Conventions dealing with child labour. Other regimes could follow this example by embedding local agreements in a nested system of authorities that balance necessary flexibility with a core of universal principles. Getting things right at the base of the system is much more important than introducing new global institutions that are divorced from their local roots—an exercise akin to building castles in the sky. Until such linkages become the norm, NGOs will continue to struggle to make connections between their work at the local and global levels.

These problems are not helped by a tendency among some NGOs to focus on global advocacy to the exclusion of the national-level processes of state-society relations that underpin the ability of any country to pursue progressive goals in an integrated economy. There is always a temptation to "leap-frog" the national arena and go directly to Washington or Brussels, where it is often easier to gain access to senior officials and achieve a response. This is understandable, but in the long term it is a serious mistake. It increases the influence of multilateral institutions over national development and erodes the process of domestic coalition-building that is essential to the development of pro-poor policy reform. In addition, the constant appearance of NGOs in international fora, combined with the dominance of NGO voices from the north, reinforces the suspicion among developing world governments that these are not genuine global alliances but yet another example of the rich world's monopoly over global debates. The NGOs concerned may see themselves as defending the interests of the poor, but it is still outsiders—not the government's own constituents—who are deciding the agenda. Most of these attacks are self-serving, but the asymmetry of NGO networks makes such criticisms inevitable. For example, only 251 of the 1550 NGOs associated with the UN Department of Public Information come from the south, and the ratio of NGOs in consultative status with ECOSOC is even lower.

Addressing this problem requires a different way of building NGO alliances, with more emphasis on horizontal relationships among equals, stronger links between local, national, and global action, and a more democratic way of deciding on strategies and messages. Jubilee 2000 (though a relatively easy case because of the absence of any south-north NGO fault-line) provides some good examples of these innovations. In Uganda, for example, a network of local NGOs have developed a dialogue with their own government on the options for debt relief, supported with technical assistance from northern NGOs like Oxfam. The results of this dialogue were then incorporated into the international debt campaign. Research has shown that NGO networks can achieve their policy goals, build capacity among NGOs in the south, *and* preserve accountability to grassroots constituents, if they consciously plan to do so from the outset and are prepared to trade off some element of speed and convenience in order to negotiate a more democratic set of outcomes. Sadly, relatively few northern NGOs seem willing to follow this approach, though, to their credit, NGOs such as Oxfam and Action Aid have started to reorient some of their resources in this direction—as with the Uganda Debt Network, cited above. Perhaps the costs seem too high, in terms of profile lost and decision-making made more complex. As we shall see, governments can help NGOs to deal with these costs and encourage them to make the transition to alliances which are less dominated by voices from the north.

From Campaign Slogans to Constituencies for Change

One of the consequences of globalization is that traditional answers to social and economic questions become redundant, or at least that the questions become more complex and the answers more uncertain. The theoretical underpinnings of pro-and anti-free-trade positions, for example, are highly contested. We cannot know in advance whether one course of action will be better than another, whatever the theory predicts. But this is a far from theoretical question; what if the NGOs who protested so loudly in Seattle turn out to be wrong in their assumptions about the future benefits that flow from different trading strategies? Returning to the issue of accountability, who pays the price? Not the NGOs themselves, but the farmers in the developing world, who will be suffering the consequences for generations. Of course, the same structures apply to pro-free-traders too, but NGOs cannot use this as a defence. All protagonists must face up to the same question: in an uncertain world, what does it mean to advocate responsibly for a predetermined position ?

Humility would be start, which is a challenge in itself to organizations used to occupying the moral high ground. More investment in research and learning is also crucial, so that the alternatives that NGOs are lobbying for can be properly grounded, tested, and critiqued. NGOs are adept at saying "no, this is wrong," but not so good at saying "yes, here is a viable alternative." Yet, a politics of pure opposition is unlikely to contribute very much to the regimes of the future. One of the consequences of this dilemma is likely to be a switch from "conversion" strategies, the traditional NGO view of advocacy, to "engagement" strategies, which aim to support a process of dialogue rather than simply lobbying for a fixed set of outcomes. This will take NGOs further into territory that may seem obvious ground—building public constituencies for policy reform—but which has thus far been largely absent from their agenda.

A strong constituency in the industrialized world is a prerequisite for the success of more equitable global regimes, new forms of governance, and the sacrifices required to alter global patterns of consumption and trade. Codes of conduct to govern multinational corporations, for example, are of little use unless they are backed by large-scale consumer pressure to enforce them. Although governments and businesses can play an important role in building these constituencies, the major responsibility is likely to fall to NGOs, since it is they who have the public trust and international connections to talk plainly and convincingly about global justice. NGOs have always talked of the need to build constituencies, but have focused on problems in the developing world instead of lifestyle, change at home, playing on the idea that "your five dollars will make the difference." It rarely does, and what would make a difference (mass-based public protest against Western indifference, for example) is never given sufficient attention. Many NGOs have cut back their public education budgets in recent years (seeing this as an overhead instead of a core activity), while government spending is only slowly resurfacing after the insularity of the Thatcher/Reagan years. A deeper engagement in constituency-building does not mean abandoning campaigns or surrendering the power of protest. But it does mean a better balance between traditional forms of NGO advocacy, and slower, longer-term work on the causes of injustice. To support this shift, NGOs will need to develop a range of new skills and competencies in public communications, and work with academics, think tanks, trade unions, and others who can help them to develop and articulate more announced positions on issues like trade and labour markets, adapted to different country contexts.

THE GROWING INTEREST OF NGOS IN MANAGEMENT

The concept of 'participatory management' has become important to development organisations. Holcombe (1995), for example, points out that many NGOs now speak of an 'empowering' or 'participatory' style of management, in which staff are seen as a source of skills and capacities, and are encouraged to take the initiative in solving problems. Moreover, Chambers (1995: 197) argues that: The institutional challenge for all development agencies is... to flatten and soften hierarchy, to develop a culture of participatory management, to recruit a gender and disciplinary mix of staff committed to people, to adopt and promote procedures, norms and rewards which permit and encourage more participation at all levels. However, despite growing interest in the concept, 'participatory management' is a term which remains both complex and unclear.

A degree of rhetoric surrounds the concept, in the same way that this is a problem for the concept of 'participation' in development (Clark, 1991). Moreover, despite the assumed tradition of participation in the management of NGOs, and the increasing popularity of 'participatory management' as a management style for NGOs, relatively little has been written on the subject.

The heightened interest in 'participatory management' must be seen, first of all, in the context of increasing importance attached to participatory development paradigms. People's participation, according to the Human Development Report (UNDP, 1993: 1), 'is becoming the central issue of our time'. Smillie (1995: 223) points out that: ... it is the NGO community through which most bilateral and multilateral agencies choose to apply participation, and from which most take their lessons.

NGOs are assumed to be participatory in approach, and this contributes to their perceived comparative advantage (Hudock, 1995). While NGOs have been examining ways to increase participation of beneficiaries in development initiatives, they have, at the same time, come under increasing pressure to 'professionalise' and, in particular, to address a widespread neglect of management. In this regard, the growth of NGOs (James, 1994), and their increasing dependence on donors for their income (Edwards and Hulme, 1992), have been important factors. Organisational growth, and the demands of donors, however, are not the only reasons for the pressure on NGOs to professionalise. Whilst NGOs have traditionally not acknowledged the link between 'internal organisational capacities and their programme performance in the field' (Sahley, 1995: 46), there is a growing realisation among them that management is a key determinant of project success (Campbell, 1987). Moreover, the growth in interest in NGO management is due, in part, to increasing organisational problems, in particular problems related to organisational growth, changes in funding, and changes in organisational role. At the same time, managers of NGOs increasingly see development as a professional practice.

One result of such pressure has been the widespread use of instruments and techniques such as Logical Framework Analysis, Objective-Oriented Project Planning (or ZOPP), Participatory Rural Assessment and Rapid Rural Assessment. It has also led to attempts to improve the administrative aspects of programme work, such as proposal writing, budgeting and reporting. Moreover, it has also resulted in a growing interest in management approaches, strategies and techniques prevalent in the business world (such as 'management by objectives', 'strategic planning', 'stakeholder-analysis', and 'mission-based management'), and a willingness to import them, often uncritically, to the world of NGOs (Smillie, 1995). The appropriateness of this latter trend, however, is questioned.

The 'NGO Management Debate'

Several researchers and consultants have applied themselves to the question of which theories and models NGO practitioners can use in the design and management of their agencies. Although it is 'still very much in its infancy' (MacKeith, 1993: 1), the tentative emergence of the study of NGO management has provided the focus for a wideranging debate about how NGOs can be more effectively organised. Indeed, there is, at present, no consensus regarding the nature of NGO management principles and practices, although the importance of management is generally accepted. Four schools of thought have been outlined by Campbell (1987) and form what I will call the 'NGO management debate'.

Three of the four perspectives presented argue that NGOs require a distinctive management style. The first school of thought insists that the critical issue is that NGOs are voluntary organisations and should draw on voluntary sector principles. A second view is that NGO contexts are critical in determining the type of management they need, and that the principles of development management should therefore strongly influence NGO management. To these schools of thought can be added a cultural perspective which questions the applicability of western management models, discusses the need for 'indigenous' approaches, and argues that the cultural environment in which the NGO operates must determine the nature of NGO management.

The arguments for a distinctive approach to NGO management, however, are not unanimously accepted. Dichter (1989), for example, argues that the distinction between the management of non-profit and commercial organisations is largely irrelevant as management principles should apply to all organisations whatever their nature and function. The priority need for NGOs, he argues, is straightforward, basic, 'nuts and bolts' management to meet equally straightforward basic weaknesses in organisational management. He points out that 'people inventions, and argues that 'means' are confused with 'ends'.

In particular, the fact that the participation of people in their own growth is a valued goal does not necessarily imply that the western management models which stress this value will be useful or appropriate in the Third World context. Such a view is echoed by DeGraaf (1987) who, while arguing that the nature of the development task does shape NGO management, insists that to say NGOs should adopt a participatory style of management because participation is important in development is over-simplistic.

'Participatory Management' and the 'NGO Management Debate'

The debate about the nature of NGO management has become polarised. In particular, to argue for a distinctive approach to the management of NGOs does not mean to reject the need for basic organisational systems (Drucker, 1990). Moreover, there are many new theories and concepts in commercial management which are very relevant to NGOs including, for example, 'strategic management', 'In Search of Excellence' management, and not least, 'participatory management' (Campbell, 1987). Secondly, the view that a participatory approach to the management of NGOs constitutes a distinctive approach is untenable, as there is a long history in the business world of employee involvement in organisational decision-making. Indeed, since the turn of the century, and particularly since the early 1960s, interest in, and support for, employee participation has been rapidly increasing (Brannen, 1983). Generic management has clearly distinguished between a taskoriented authoritarian approach to management, on the one hand, and an employee centred, democratic or participative style on the other (Vroom and Jago, 1988).

'Empowerment' is now widely used in business and management as well as in development (Wright, 1994), and 'participative management', such as that proposed by Likert's (1961) 'System 4', is a recognised approach to management. In particular, Japanese corporations such Hitachi, Nissan, Honda, Mitsubishi and Toyota are often cited as exemplars of employee-participatory practices. At the same time, forms of employee participation have flourished in the 1980s in the guise of managerial policy initiatives inspired by the new 'excellence' movement, and have been expounded as a key instrument in the creation of Human Resource Management (HRM) strategies. Finally, in recent years, inspired by Japanese management practice, various forms of team-working based around customer care and Total Quality Management (TQM) programmes have witnessed a considerable rise in popularity.

THE APPROPRIATENESS OF 'PARTICIPATORY MANAGEMENT' FOR NGOS

The NGO management debate has attempted to address the question: what style of management is appropriate for NGOs? In so doing, the debate is valuable. However, given that participation in decision-making is a feature of governmental and commercial organisations, the association of a participatory style of management with a distinctive approach to NGO management is unhelpful. It is more useful to examine the advantages of participation to organisations generally, and to NGOs in particular, and then identify those factors in the NGO context which make a participatory approach more appropriate for them.

There are a number of perspectives on the increasing interest in participation in the commercial sector. Guest and Knight (1979) argue that it represents part of the search for... a new means of overcoming industrial and economic problems, changing market conditions internationally, rising expectations of the workforce, and interest in the concept of industrial democracy. The emphasis on changing environmental conditions is taken up by Lawler (1986: 19) who insists that 'the societal, business, product, and work force changes that have occurred argue strongly for a change in management style', and who believes that 'in most situations some form of participative management is the best answer' (Lawler, 1986: 11). At the same time, Wall and Lischeron (1977: 1) point out that in contemporary society 'participation, in one form or another, is seen as one means of improving the quality of working life'.

However, thc increased interest in participation cannot simply be seen as stemming from changed contextual factors and a desire for greater work humanisation. An instrumental view of participation-that greater participation will lead to greater efficiency, and consequently greater profits-is fundamental in the commercial sector (Beardwell and Holden, 1994), and is particularly reflected in the 'hard', rather than the 'soft' approach to Human Resource Management (Storey, 1987).8 That participation is linked to improved performance is evident from Ouchi (1981) who states: Decision-making by consensus has been the subject of a great deal of research in Europe and the United States over the past twenty years, and the evidence strongly suggests that a consensus approach yields more creative decisions and more effective implementation than does individual decision-making. Moreover, the participation of staff is inextricably linked with the concept of 'learning organisations'. Senge (1990: 3), for example, argues that 'the organisations that will truly excel in the future will be the organisations that discover how to tap people's commitment and capacity to learn at all levels of an organisation'. 'Participatory management' and 'participatory development' As noted earlier, several authors argue that a participatory approach to management is particularly suitable for NGOs whose work involves the promotion of participation and the empowerment of beneficiaries. Chambers (1983: 210), for example, insists that such a management style is more in keeping with 'bottom-up development' or a participatory development approach. NGOs require a 'new professionalism' based on fundamental 'reversals' in the values, attitudes and behaviour of NGO staff, so that the people whom the NGO aims to support are truly empowered. Carroll's (1992: 205) study of NGOs in Latin America demonstrates that an open, collegial management style builds confidence and trust among beneficiaries and support organisations, and is, therefore, a key organisational quality for promoting popular participation. Similarly, the British Overseas Development Administration points out that 'culture, management structure, goals and sources of funding, all influence the manner and extent to which an aid agency can enhance the participation of other stakeholders' (Eyben, 1994: 4.3). Indeed, Roche (1992: 188) argues:

Experience suggests that a decentralised structure with semiautonomous, self-managed federated units, coupled with information and cooperative learning, is perhaps the most appropriate organisational design for supporting micro-development. A second theme that emerges in the literature is that NGOs need to develop decentralised and participatory decision-making structures, and adopt a problemsolving rather than a predictive blue-print approach to management, to ensure flexibility and maintain the ability to adapt to constantly changing realities.

In particular, participatory planning processes are important as it is the field staff who normally have closest contact with beneficiaries (Sahley, 1995). This 'effectiveness' argument is also taken up, for example, by Brodhead and Herbert-Copley (1988), who suggest that

NGOs must adopt a participatory approach in order to have wider impact.

A third theme which emerges is the expectations of NGO staff. Clark (1991: 61), for example, states that: NGO staff are generally highly committed to their work because of widely shared values and a belief in the social change mission inherent in their work. This generates a sense of ownership which, when combined with the widespread expectation that organisations promoting democracy and participation should themselves be democratic, means that 'an autocratic style simply wouldn't work: the staff require participation'.

Moreover, Hodson (1992: 135) argues that as NGOs grow 'decentralised and consensual forms of decision-making' are of particular importance 'if decisions are to be seen by staff as legitimate'. In addition, there is an assumption that respect for workers leads to improved organisational functioning. Clark, (1991: 62), for example, suggests: Naturally an organisation of principled and committed workers will function best if staff feel respected, and listened to.

The 'NGO management debate' cannot be easily resolved. In particular, a number of questions about the appropriateness of a participatory style of management for NGOs remain unanswered. Moreover, the debate about the appropriateness of 'participatory management' is constrained by a degree of definitional ambiguity which needs to be addressed.

A Case Study of Concern Mozambique

The aim of the case study is to explore the reasons why CONCERN Mozambique is seeking to adopt a more participatory style of management and to outline the proposals which emerged about the direction such change might take. The process of change in CONCERN Mozambique is underpinned by a number of assumptions made by management staff about the importance of participation, and its role in the management of an organisation committed to promoting participatory development. These are as follows:

A 'Natural' Approach for Participatory Development?

In the first place, the consensus among interviewees is that CONCERN's commitment to participatory development necessitates a participatory style of management. Such a management style is considered, for example, to be 'a natural approach', given that the organisation is committed to promoting participation in its development programmes. As one Programme Manager stated: You cannot do participatory development without participatory management.

In particular, it was noted that an organisation must practise what it preaches, and that since CONCERN Worldwide is promoting participation of the beneficiaries, the participation of staff is therefore essential. As another Programme Manager remarked: One can't expect staff to mobilise, animate and facilitate interest groups to analyse their own problems and set their own objectives if the organisation does not have a similar empowering approach with staff.

Programme Responsiveness

Secondly, there is among programme management a widespread belief that greater participation of staff, and particularly field-workers, in the management of the organisation will result in improved programme responsiveness. This view is reflected in the 'CONCERN

Mozambique Policy Framework' (1995) which states: As an agency that targets the poorest we need a management style that is flexible and responsive to the needs of the poor. A participatory management style enables those staff who are closest to the poor, those at project operational level, to guide the organisation in its programme design and implementation to allow the needs of the poor to be identified and met. Furthermore, the interviews with the Country Director reveal a fundamental belief that staff at project level are in the best position to make decisions for that project. This view is echoed by one interviewee who remarked: We get reality in decisions... if people further down the line are involved in the decision-making.

Staff Empowerment

At the same time, the general view is that 'participatory management' is not just about involving staff, but about 'empowering' them, and creating 'voice'. As the Country Director remarked: CONCERN is here to deliver a service. The most important people in that service delivery are the field workers (they are the most important people in the organisation in many ways). Space has to be made for those people to have a voice in the organisation. While most programme management staff spoke about 'participatory management' resulting in improved decision-making and ownership of decisions, a number of Programme Managers also suggested that 'participatory management' is an appropriate management style given that CONCERN Mozambique is committed to building up local staff capacity, and in particular, to creating the conditions necessary for sustainable development.

Better 'Downward' Accountability

'Participatory management' is also seen as enhancing

'downward accountability'. This is evident from the 'CONCERN Mozambique Policy Framework' (1995) which incorporates the idea, originally suggested by CONCERN Worldwide's Southern Africa Division (correspondence, September 1995), that teams and teamwork at management and project level will 'avoid the emergence of a tall hierarchical structure between the target group and field management' and, more especially, will 'ensure that field resources are not diverted away from the poorest'.

Promoting Democracy

Finally, while Programme Managers, in general, see 'participatory management' in terms of its having a crucial role in improving organisational effectiveness, the wider implications of adopting a participatory style of management were noted by one Programme Manager who commented on the importance, in a fledgling democracy, as Mozambique is, of promoting democracy within the workplace. In summary, the case study suggests that while a number of different reasons may be identified, they are all related to the ultimate aim of improved development practice, and in particular, are inspired by a fundamental commitment to participatory development.

IMPROVED DEVELOPMENT PRACTICE

Participatory management is seen therefore not as an end in itself, but as means of reaching organisational goals more effectively. As one senior staff member commented: The only reason we have participatory management is to facilitate our development approach. It is not for its own sake. The study revealed the crucial role of leadership. It is clear that, on a practical level, CONCERN Mozambique has initiated this process of institutional change because the Country Director strongly believes in the importance of such an approach, and more significantly, has acted on that belief by taking advantage of a number of opportunities which have enabled the process to take place.

The most important of these has been the support for the initiative from CONCERN Southern Africa Division, including its willingness to allow the budget flexibility necessary for the development of the new systems. At the same time, according to the Country Director, that this belief is shared by the Programme Managers and key national staff has also been crucial, as has their willingness to accept the new responsibilities that a participatory style of management involves.

The case study indicates, in the first place, that management staff in CONCERN Mozambique clearly see 'participatory management' not as a collection of tools and techniques, but as a fundamental approach to management.

At the same time, it is understood as something which must be created, or allowed to evolve, over time: as one Programme Manager pointed out, it is essentially a process of 'introducing things bit by bit'. Secondly, though the possibility of including other stakeholders had been briefly discussed, the general understanding among CONCERN programme management staff is that 'participatory management' is, for the time being at least, only about the greater involvement of staff members, and in particular field staff, in decision-making.

It is therefore perceived as overlapping with, but distinct from, CONCERN Mozambique's commitment to 'participatory development', which pledges it to securing 'the participation of interested parties in all stages of the programming process-government, team, target groups, informal structures etc.' At the same time, 'participatory management' is not seen as representing in any way a rejection, or diminution, of standards of professionalism and accountability. There have been no changes to the financial or administrative systems, nor are any intended, and auditing and input control remain crucial. Indeed, at a meeting of senior programme staff with the Southern Africa Regional Director in March 1995 it was agreed that 'by ensuring that tasks are better defined, such control mechanisms can be enhanced by participatory objective-led planning'. These changes also require a firm hand. 'Participatory management' is not about the adoption of an unstructured, 'laissez-faire' style of management. On the contrary, it is seen (though not always positively) as quite procedural, and very structured. As the Country Director remarked:

Participatory management is not less structured; it is more structured if anything. It's quite prescribed, but people are involved in the prescription.

Finally, 'participatory management' is linked to a 'reversal' in the way in which the organisation is conceptualised and represented. In the first place, it is informed by an understanding of the organisation as directly related to, and in service of, the beneficiaries (who are conceived of as 'clients'). In addition, it is underpinned by a view of the NGO as a 'bottom-up' organisation in which the most important members are those closest to the clients. The present CONCERN Mozambique organogram, which is based on the concept of an 'inverted triangle', reflects these views.

The study also reveals that there is a crucial link between the adoption of a more participatory style of management and institutional change. Indeed, as one

Programme Manager remarked: A participatory approach to development requires changes at all levels of the organisation.

The resulting programme proposals CONCERN Mozambique's commitment to such change is evident in the five programme proposals, each of which states: CONCERN Mozambique is going through a process of institutional change aimed at creating a management style that is conducive to the type of community development programme being proposed here. These changes commenced in 1994 and are still ongoing, are structural and cultural in nature, and have taken several forms.

A 'Flatter' Organisation

'Participatory management' is clearly identified with the creation of a 'flatter' or more 'horizontal' form of management, and the reduction in the layers of authority between senior management and field-workers. This facilitates speedier and more participatory decision-making, and is assumed to increase programme responsiveness. Additionally, it narrows the gap between the organisation's target group and senior management.

Secondly, the study reveals that the adoption of a team approach, both at project and country levels, is central to the style of management adopted by CONCERN Mozambique. A project team (referred to as a 'General Assembly') has been formed in each of the five programme areas, and is the most important aspect of the new structure at project level. Comprising all staff directly involved in project activities, it meets every three months.

Its responsibilities include the design of work plans using the ZOPP methodology, the evaluation and re-design of existing methodologies, and the evaluation of the management team. Furthermore, two new fora have been established at country level, and meet annually: a 'Wider Group', which is concerned with national policy and strategy, and a 'Steering Committee', which is responsible for ensuring that policy is implemented.

The study also reveals that adoption of a more participatory style of management is not just about changing organisational structures. It is also clearly seen to involve the creation of an environment in which dialogue, communication, and particularly organisational learning, are facilitated and encouraged. The establishment of the staff magazine, in June 1995, is an important development in this regard. Furthermore, the conducting of an evaluation, by the staff in early 1996, of CONCERN Mozambique's strengths and weaknesses during the previous year, and the publication of the results in the staff magazine, reflect the link between 'participatory management' and a commitment to the development of a culture of openness.

Levels of Participation

The study confirms that, in CONCERN Mozambique, staff are now more involved in both project and country management. This parallels 'participative management' practices at 'shop-floor' and 'plant' levels (Guest and Knight, 1979). Moreover, the involvement of employees at country management level, in decisions that relate to the entire country programme rather than just projects, illustrates that the participation of staff in CONCERN Mozambique is, to use Strauss and Rosenstein's (1970) framework, both 'immediate' and 'distant'. At the same time, however, the adoption of a participatory style of management does not, for the time being at least, imply the participation of non-management staff in decision-making at levels higher than the Mozambique country programme.

Secondly, the study reveals that the participation of staff in the design of work is perceived by senior staff as central to 'participatory management'. In this regard, the ZOPP methodology, introduced in 1995, is crucial. As the Country Director remarked:

> ZOPP is at the core of participatory management: it gives staff a language, puts people on an equal footing, and gives people the confidence and the skills to sit with their boss and argue.

At the same time, 'participatory management' is understood to involve more that just the design of work. Four of the eleven field-workers surveyed, for instance, mentioned their involvement in deciding the responsibilities, tasks and procedures of the project team as an example of the way in which they are now more involved in decisionmaking. Indeed, staff are increasingly invited to participate in decisions about work conditions (for example, staff salaries and benefits) as well as in decisions about administrative issues (such as staff appraisal, staff selection, and transport policy).

The study also reveals that there are different degrees or 'intensities' of participation within CONCERN Mozambique, and suggests that 'participatory management' is more than just improved information-sharing and greater consultation of staff. More authority has been delegated than previously, and indeed, there has been, and continues to be, a transfer of power. However, the degree to which this takes place varies according to situational factors, and more particularly, occurs within carefully defined parameters. The study also suggests that the intensity of participation depends not only on the level of the decision-making, but on the nature of the decision. The decision-making power of the Steering Committee is a good example: Moreover, when looking at areas of decision-making not related to the design of work, there has, to date, been more in terms of consultation than delegation. This is indicated by the results of the focus group discussion with the national staff of the Maputo office, during which staff were asked to identify recent decisions made and staff participation in them.

In summary, the case study has shown that CONCERN Mozambique has commenced a process of institutional change aimed at facilitating its development approach. This process is still emerging, and is inspired by a fundamental commitment to providing a better service to organisational beneficiaries. Important lessons can be learned from this experience, and these will be the subject of the next and final chapter.

EMERGING ISSUES

Important practical issues are raised by the case study of 'participatory management' in CONCERN Mozambique. In the first place, the case reveals that the initiative in CONCERN Mozambique is primarily an attempt to arrange internal structures and procedures in such a way as to most effectively and efficiently undertake the organisation's tasks and purposes. In this regard its objectives may be no different from the objectives of 'participative management' in the commercial sector. However, the aim of organisational efficiency in NGOs is not the making of profits, as it is in the commercial sector, but improved service to the NGOs' beneficiaries or clients.

At the same time, the case study also reveals the importance of a 'process orientation' in NGO management, and suggests that the nature of the task has an important, if not a crucial role, in determining organisational processes. It suggests that attention to 'process', or what Paton (1991) calls the 'expressive aspect of management', may be of greater significance for NGOs, particularly those involved in the promotion of participation. 'Participatory management' may therefore represent a conscious effort to exercise management authority and responsibility in ways which are consistent with the broader social values and purposes of the NGO. In particular, it may be seen as an attempt to address the management challenges that the task of promoting participation imposes on an organisation. As Batsleer (1995) points out, however, none of this is new among voluntary organisations.

The study also suggests that at the heart of the task dimension of 'participatory management' is the assumption that the participation of staff leads to improved decision-making and, therefore, greater effectiveness. This is not new, however, either in NGO management or management generally. In the NGO context, it has been explored by Carroll (1992) whose study of NGOs in Latin America concluded that effective NGOs use a participatory style which relies on local knowledge and dialogue with beneficiary groups, and have a less hierarchical and more collegial internal organisation than public or private organisations.

However, that greater staff participation will lead to improved decision-making, and that this in turn will result in more responsive programmes, are both assumptions which need to be tested. As a consequence, an important aspect of the relationship between 'participatory management' and improved development practice remains unproven. At the same time, the study highlights the close connection between 'participatory management' and organisational learning, which is increasingly promoted as crucial to organisational effectiveness.

The case study also suggests that 'participatory management' is not necessarily concerned with increasing staff motivation. However, the study also suggests that 'participatory management' may be a strategy which effectively capitalises on expectations among staff throughout the organisation who, according to Sahley (1995: 52), 'need to feel that they can contribute to the development of policy and strategy'.

At the same time, a participatory style of management may be bolstered by a ' view of staff relations-which assumes that management and employees are working to the same goal of the organisation's success (Fincham and Rhodes, 1992). Secondly, it is clear that management staff in CONCERN Mozambique see 'participatory management' largely, though not exclusively, in terms of its benefits to the organisation, rather than to staff.

While such an instrumental view is dominant in the generic management literature, the participation of staff may, nonetheless, be seen as an end in itself. As noted earlier, 'participative management' may have as its objective the improvement of the 'quality of working life', or the promotion of industrial democracy. That these are not explicit concerns of the management in CONCERN Mozambique suggests, however, that 'participatory management' may be seen in the context of the 'hard' rather than the 'soft' side of Human Resource Management (Storey, 1987).

The study also indicates that different objectives may

be attributed to 'participatory management' even within the same organisation. In addition, different aspects of the process of adopting a participatory style of management may be associated with different objectives.

One of the implications is that the perceived 'success' or 'failure' of 'participatory management' will depend on the aims attributed to the greater involvement of staff in decision-making. Consequently, the question: 'Is Participatory Management effective?' has no simple answer. At the same time, the study suggests that there is a danger that a participatory approach to management may be perceived by NGO staff as appropriate only to those NGOs involved in 'participatory development'. However, the generic management literature clearly suggests the advantages to organisations, generally, of increased employee participation.

Issues for Researchers

While the case study suggests that 'participatory management' may represent a distinctive approach for NGOs, it also reveals that such an approach to management is not fundamentally different from management approaches adopted by some organisations in other sectors. Indeed, the adoption of participatory styles of management among NGOs may be seen as part of the tradition of importing management concepts, prevalent in the business world, to the NGO sector. At the same time, the study demonstrates that NGOs may learn a great deal from for-profit organisations about the importance and nature of participation in management. The case study also confirms the view that 'participatory management' is more than a collection of participatory techniques and involves institutional change that is both structural and cultural in nature. It implies a pro-active 'formalisation', or 'institutionalisation' of participation, so that existing patterns of participation are transformed into structures of participation. Such structures are necessarily expressions of the organisation's fundamental and long-term commitment to a participatory process. 'Participatory management' can be seen, therefore, in the context of the challenge facing NGOs to lose their 'shyness' of management and take on a strategic management orientation rather than focusing on logistics or project management (Korten, 1987: 155). At the same time, the study shows that translating a policy commitment to participation on the part of the organisation into a meaningful set of strategic and operational choices may be problematic. In particular, there is an inherent irony in promoting participation from the top down.

The case study demonstrates that the concepts and categories used to describe participation in the generic literature are of considerable use in understanding the nature of participation in NGO management. In particular, it reveals that 'participatory management' in NGOs is a multi-dimensional and multi-faceted concept, and is no less complex than participation in commercial organisations. Participatory schemes may pervade many or all levels of the organisation, and may take different forms. Moreover, the study endorses the view, expressed by the British Overseas Development Administration, that 'from any stakeholder's perspective participation may be seen as a spectrum model with a range of possibilities from being manipulated to being in control' (Eyben, 1994: 2.1).

The participation of staff will, therefore, vary in intensity according, for example, to the nature of the work, the experience and capability of staff, and the stage of development of the organisation. In this respect, White's

(1995) conceptual framework, which argues that participation may by 'nominal', 'instrumental', 'representative' or 'transformative' (with only the final category truly empowering), may usefully be applied to, and inform, our understanding of 'participatory management'. While interest in participation in the management of commercial organisations is generally confined to the involvement of employees, the study reveals that participation in the management of development NGOs may refer to the involvement, not just of staff, but of other stakeholders, even the beneficiaries.

'Participatory management' may thus be seen in the context of an NGO's attempt to structurally and systematically engage its multiple stakeholders (Fowler, 1995). However, the study also suggests that, in practice, participation in the management of NGOs may be confined to the greater involvement of NGO staff. This is in accordance with the view that the involvement of beneficiaries in the management of the organisation may not be feasible (Clark, 1991). In this regard, 'participatory management' may differ little from employee participation in the commercial sector.

There is no trade-off between greater participation of staff in decision-making and maintaining high standards of professionalism. It demonstrates that 'participatory management' does not mean being non-directive, and, somewhat paradoxically, requires strong leadership. Indeed, it suggests the accuracy of Clark's (1991: 66) view that achieving the right balance between strong leadership, which ensures resolute pursuit of strong ideas, and openness of style, which ensures that all staff feel properly valued, is the greatest management challenge for NGOs, particularly as they grow in size. 'Participatory management' inevitably raises questions about the nature of the relationship between those who manage and those who are managed. Such debate has been vigorous in the commercial sector throughout this century (Beardwell and Holden, 1994: 6). In particular, 'participatory management' implies a conception of the organisation as an environment in which managerial discretion is permitted freer rein, and staff are given greater 'voice' (Hirschmann, 1970). As such, it is essentially no different from 'participative management' in the commercial sector in which employees are enabled, to varying degrees, to have a greater say in decision-making (Beardwell and Holden, 1994).

The case also demonstrates that 'participatory management' may represent a management style in which 'worker empowerment' in practice takes place very much within the boundaries set by management. In this regard, too, it is no different from employee involvement practice in the commercial sector. At the same time, there is likely to be a dilemma, within management, in terms of how much power to extend to the workforce. Management will want to harness the workers' creative energies, but at the same time not undermine managerial prerogatives, particularly accountability. 'Participatory management' may be seen, therefore, as an attempt to reconcile the tension between participatory ideology and the hierarchical requirements of institutional action (Martinez Nogueira, 1987).

The research also highlights the important link between a more participatory style of management and democracy within the organisation. It suggests the accuracy of Pateman's (1970) argument that it is possible for 'partial' participation at both immediate and distant levels to take place without a democratisation of authority structures, and that 'full' participation may be introduced at the lower level within the context of a non-democratic structure overall. However, while it may be possible for a more participatory approach to be introduced within an organisation which is not participatory in management style, the case suggests that official endorsement (at the organisational or 'company' level) is essential if such practices are to be legitimised, and therefore truly 'formalised' and 'institutionalised'.

The importance of a gender focus in 'participatory management' needs to be made explicit. In the first place, 'participatory management' requires an examination of popular assumptions about the position of women in organisations. Secondly, as Goetz (1995) points out, unless women and men are represented equally at all levels of an organisation, management can never be truly 'participatory'. Moreover, an organisation whose management is not gender equitable will ultimately fail to address the priorities of women, who, as Kabeer (1994) points out, have been and continue to be marginalised by deeply entrenched, and hence barely visible, biases in development theory and practice.

'Participatory management' must be informed by culture and, like any management approach, must 'spring from the cultural values which govern social interactions and dominate intra-and inter-organisational relations'. However, culture is an extremely complex phenomenon (Wright, 1994), and although writers such as Hofstede (1980) and Laurent (1983) have attempted to examine the influence of cultural factors on management generally, our understanding of such factors remains unclear. The treatment of the relationship between participatory styles of management and culture, therefore, needs careful investigation. In particular, the idea that 'participatory management', as a people-centred approach, is a western construct (Dichter, 1989), and therefore foreign to Third World contexts, needs to be seriously challenged.

While 'participatory management' and 'participatory development' are sometimes used interchangeably, the study suggests that this is a terminological rather than a conceptual problem. For senior management staff in CONCERN Mozambique the distinction is clearly unproblematic. 'Participatory development' is clearly about the involvement of beneficiaries in the planning, implementation and evaluation of external interventions. 'Participatory management', on the other hand, is about the participation of staff (and possibly other stakeholders) not only in the design of organisational activities, but in decisions about organisational policy, strategy and operations. It is essential, therefore, to avoid confusing the terms, and in particular, to link the two more precisely. What emerges from the study, but is not discussed in the literature, is the degree to which 'participatory management' may be highly formal and procedural. In particular, it requires the transformation of existing patterns of participation into formalised structures. Ironically, this may result in stronger managerial control. At the same time, the study suggests that the structured and controlled nature of 'participatory management' may strengthen rather than weaken accountability.

In particular, it may support programming, monitoring and evaluation systems which are important 'downward' accountability instruments (Wils, 1995). The case also suggests that 'participatory management' is an aspirational concept, and thus may be best described, in the Weberian sense, as an 'ideal type'.

It indicates that the degree to which any organisation may facilitate the greater involvement of non-managerial staff in decisionmaking is inevitably limited, and will be contingent on the complex interplay of a number of organisational variables. Moreover, like other management approaches such as Total Quality Management, 'participatory management' will remain open to a variety of definitions and interpretations. As a result, NGOs will need to create their own model of 'participatory management'. This, however, is not necessarily a constraint.

Finally, the case study also suggests that 'participatory management' must be seen in the context of Campbell's (1987: 3) assertion that 'there is not, nor can there be, only one correct way of managing an organisation'.

This 'contingency approach', which is the dominant approach to the management of organisations generally (Child, 1988), must be the context within which 'participatory management' is discussed. In this way, 'participatory management' can be completely consistent with Dichter's (1989) view that what is needed is not a search for universal principles but a clearer focus on the actual field conditions, as it is these which must determine which management style is appropriate.

10

INGOs' Accountability

International NGOs have structurally weaker accountability mechanisms than the other sectors in that there are less formal mechanisms imposing accountability from the outside. NGOs, for example, can not claim that they democratically represent the groups they advocate for, unlike democratic governments who can point to open electoral processes. Nor can they claim their services are accountable as a result of market consumer choice, however weak this argument may be.

Beneficiaries, NGOs' nearest equivalent to consumers, are often the most marginalized groups within a society and are not in a position to reject programmes and services if they are substandard. This leaves the sector highly open to criticism.

It would be wrong, however, to suggest that no structural mechanisms exist within the sector. State regulation and institutional donor-driven reporting, for example, provide mechanisms of accountability. Unfortunately, they do not translate up to the global level or ignore certain stakeholders, like NGOs' beneficiaries. States tend to regulate around disclosure of NGO financial information and governance structures. Like the corporate sector, this is limited to the national arena only. No international law exists for the regulation of INGOs and there are wide ranging debates as to whether such a law would be appropriate given the large diversity of organizations that fall under the nongovernmental umbrella. A limited number of codes and standards are emerging at the global level. Interestingly, many of these draw on existing global accountability standards within the corporate and governmental sector, focusing primarily on reporting. For example, the Corporate Responsibility Campaign, which looks into social and environmental reporting, prides itself on applying its standards to corporations and NGOs alike.

An absence of structural accountability mechanisms does not mean that NGOs are necessarily less accountable. For example, the NGO sector leads on consulting with less powerful stakeholders like its beneficiaries before, during and even after it has undertaken project work, even without formal mechanisms imposing such accountability (Neligan et al, 2003). The reason behind this is largely the sector's use of participatory development practices, which stress the need to empower beneficiaries to make their own choices and decide their own futures in order for effective development to take place. Engaging with beneficiaries is even becoming the case in the humanitarian emergency sector, despite the difficulties posed by the environment in undertaking this activity. Although INGOs lead in this area, it should be stressed that engagement is largely confined to the grassroots level in relation to projects and programmes, and is not replicated at the national, regional or international level of the organization. Nor is there much engagement around advocacy work.

PUBLIC AWARENESS OF ACCOUNTABILITY FAILINGS

The absence of effective accountability mechanisms at the global level has produced a worrying disconnection between global organizations and the individuals they impact. This has been cited by many academics, but also by numerous citizens, who increasingly feel the impact of global organizations in their daily lives, but have little ability to have their voices heard, much to their frustration. More and more individuals around the world are calling for greater accountability at the global level, with a need for all organizations to listen and respond, including those once deemed immune from scrutiny. Intergovernmental organizations are facing ever-increasing scrutiny from wide sections of the population. Organizations as diverse as the OECD, the World Bank and the WTO have all been targeted by highly vocal civil society campaigns over the last couple of years. These campaigns often challenge not only the substance of the IGOs' policy decisions, but also the very processes by which IGO decisions are taken. Just as IGOs' accountability has been put under the spotlight, so has that of corporations. It is perhaps no wonder, given the extraordinary financial muscle of TNCs and their high visibility in terms of global branding. Until recently, calls for greater INGO accountability had been limited, with the sector viewed as essentially benign. Over the last couple of years this has changed, with a dramatic growth in the number of people voicing concerns. There is no single explanation for this growth in concern, but clearly it must be linked to the increasing financial and political impact of the sector.

In 2002, NGOs turned over an estimated US$1 trillion globally, providing vital services to individuals and communities around the world (Sustainability, 2003) INGOs also have an increasingly powerful voice, running campaigns on matters such as environmental degradation, workers' rights and trade rules, which corporations and governments ignore at their peril.In addition, the nature of INGO work has also stimulated questions concerning their accountability. Many INGOs have taken on the role of monitoring the accountability of governments and corporations on behalf of citizens around the world. Recently, Christian Aid wrote a report on the 'real face' of corporate responsibility (Christian Aid, 2004). This level of critical review of the accountability of others has left INGOs exposed to questions surrounding their own accountability. This could be one of the biggest internal drivers for the sector to tackle this issue, as INGOs themselves realize that it is no longer tenable to demand accountability within other sectors without addressing it within their own. It is also, as noted later on in this chapter, one of the reasons why the issue of NGO accountability is so highly politicized.

THE ONE WORLD TRUST'S GLOBAL ACCOUNTABILITY PROJECT

- A new approach to accountability is required that recognizes the complexity of accountability and the diversity of stakeholders' needs. In 2000, the One World Trust (OWT) launched the Global Accountability Project (GAP). The project promotes greater accountability of global organizations. It does so by highlighting the key mechanisms that enhance the accountability of three main types of global organizations-intergovernmental, TNCs and INGOs, assessing the accountability of representative organizations within these three sectors, identifying accountability gaps and advocating for reforms on specific accountability issues. Through GAP, the OWT has developed a new model of accountability that identifies some core elements of accountability applicable to all types of global organizations. Before describing these elements in detail, it is important to explore how the Trust defines or perceives accountability. Central to the Trust's model of accountability is the notion of the stakeholder whereby the right to hold an organization or individual to account is granted to 'any group or individuals who can affect or is affected by... an organization' (Freeman, 1984). The model, therefore, firmly places itself within the modern approaches to accountability, valuing a wide array of stakeholders. In fact, OWT employs a new categorization of stakeholders, employing the terms internal and external stakeholders. 'Internal stakeholders' refers to stakeholders who are directly linked to the organization and who often have formal powers to hold an organization to account. This group often has the power to impose accountability on an organization, although not always. 'External stakeholders' refers more to those stakeholders that are affected by an organization's work, but are not formally part of it, like the NGO's beneficiaries. External stakeholders tend to be less powerful and unable to exert their rights. The Trust's emphasis is on empowering those stakeholders that are less powerful and ensuring they have the ability to hold organizations to account. The categorization is not definitive and many stakeholders move from being external to internal and vice versa.

The Trust's definition of accountability also recognizes that accountability is not only a means through which individuals and organizations are held responsible for their actions, but it is also a means by which organizations can take internal responsibility for shaping their organizational mission and values, for opening themselves to external scrutiny and for assessing performance in relation to goals. It engages with both the sanctioning elements of accountability and the often negated learning and participatory aspects.

The GAP model recognizes that there are two complementary elements to accountability: on the one hand, international organizations have a responsibility to engage all their stakeholders in their decision-making and to be transparent about their actions; on the other hand, all stakeholders should also have the power to impose some sort of sanctions if organizations fail to comply with their stated objectives. Their notion of accountability extends beyond traditional mechanisms of oversight, monitoring or auditing by adding some element of control, exposure and potential redress.

ELABORATING THE GAP MODEL OF ACCOUNTABILITY

The GAP model of accountability identifies four core dimensions that make an organization more accountable to its stakeholders. These must be integrated into an organization's policies, processes and practices at all levels and stages of decision-making and implementation, in relationships with both its internal and external stakeholders.

These four dimensions are: transparency, participation, evaluation, and complaints and reddress. The higher the quality and level of embeddedness of these dimensions in all organizational policies, processes and practices, the more accountable the organization is. These four dimensions are connected with and impact on each other, thus highlighting how fundamental each and every single one of them is to the accountability of organizations. They are summarized in the table above.

THE GAP ACCOUNTABILITY MODEL

Transparency: Transparency implies a free flow of information: processes are directly accessible to stakeholders and enough information is provided to understand and monitor them. This dimension covers the degree of information provided by organizations to the public, exploring access to internal decision-making through information on an organization's mission, activities and finances.

Participation: Participation refers to the degree to which organizations involve their stakeholders (internal and external) at all levels of decision-making within the organization. It covers not only internal governance issues, looking at, for example, the representativeness, transparency and degree of control governing and executive boards have over an organization, but also the extent to which an organization engages with external stakeholders via consultations and partnerships at both project and policy levels.

Evaluation: This dimension refers to the existence and effectiveness of tools and procedures that are in place to evaluate an organization's performance. It recognizes the need for two types of evaluations to help an organization increase its accountability-internal evaluations (carried out by staff assessing their own work) and external evaluations (where information is evaluated by a competent independent authority). Tools of evaluation can be combined with processes of participation to develop external downward accountability mechanisms through systematic involvement of stakeholders in evaluating organizations. Complaints and This dimension refers to 'the mechanisms through which an organization enables its stakeholders (both internal and external) to address complaints against its decisions and actions, and through which it ensures that these complaints are properly reviewed and acted upon' (De Las Casas, 2005). Enabling stakeholders to bring complaints against an organization is a critical aspect of accountability.

Through participatory methods involving a wide range of academics, policy-makers and practitioners, One World Trust is undertaking research to identify the principles and guidelines of each of the dimensions. Quantitative and qualitative indicators have been developed for each of the dimensions, in order to offer users a more practical understanding of how accountability can be operationalized.

GLOBAL ACCOUNTABILITY REPORT IN RELATION TO INGOS

In 2003, the Trust released its first report entitled Power without Accountability? (Kovach et al, 2003). The report assessed the accountability of 18 organizations from the intergovernmental, corporate and international non-governmental sector using an earlier version of its accountability model. It focused on two of the key dimensions identified in the model: participation and transparency. However, it only developed indicators for assessing and measuring partial aspects of these dimensions. In the case of participation, the report focused on examining the representativeness of internal governing structures and exploring the make-up of the governing and executive boards. In terms of transparency, the report assessed online information only, looking at the degree to which internal decision-making information was made available, as well as at the financial data and evaluation reports.

The report controversially ranked organizations according to the results it found. Overall, two clear conclusions emerged from the report. First, in terms of governance, the report found that INGOs had fairer and more representative governing structures at the board level than other global organizations, ensuring that a minority of stakeholders did not dominate decision-making. Second, in terms of transparency, the report showed that INGOs were not that transparent, especially in comparison to both the corporate and the intergovernmental sector. This finding was picked up by many in the media and some of the organizations assessed, especially those that had been subject to calls that they were not accountable. The next sections will briefly summarize the findings of the report in relation to INGOs only, providing additional commentary and, at times, critical thoughts on the findings. Finally, it explores the impact of the report's findings in the media and policy-making circles, highlighting the highly political nature of NGO accountability.

INGO GOVERNANCE: REPRESENTATIVE?

International NGOs, like all other organizations, have a governing and an executive body. The governing body is composed of representatives from all of the national member organizations who are part of the INGO's federal and con-federal structure. At the executive level, INGOs face the same tensions as IGOs as they try to ensure both efficiency (that is, small executives) and fair member representation. The report highlighted that most INGOs have resolved the dilemma successfully by appointing small executives and employing mechanisms to ensure fair representation of members within them. This is unlike IGOs, who have tended to let a small minority of members (in this case nation states) dominate. Five of the seven INGOs in the study opted for a smaller executive than their governing body and all but one of these ensured that a minority of members were not over-represented. The International Chamber of Commerce (ICC) was the exception. Most INGOs employed geographical formulas to ensure that different regions were fairly represented at the executive level and no one region could dominate (Amnesty International, International Confederation of Free Trade Unions (ICFTU)). Only CARE International and Oxfam International represented all national member organizations directly on the executive. The dilemma was reduced for them because they were small confederations, each made up of 12 members.

It also appeared that a minority of members did not dominate decisionmaking in any of the INGOs studied as a result of an unfair distribution of voting rights. Four of the INGOs distributed their votes equally among their members: CARE International, Oxfam International, the International Federation of the Red Cross and Red Crescent Societies (IFRC) and the World Wide Fund for Nature (WWF). Amnesty International, the ICC and the ICFTU distributed votes in relation to the size and financial contribution of members. However, a lack of transparency with the ICFTU and ICC over the distribution of votes to members made it difficult to tell whether a minority of members actually held a majority of votes. Only Amnesty International provided this information and it revealed that a minority did not dominate. For all of the INGOs, however, changes to the governing articles must be decided by a supermajority, preventing a small cabal of members from blocking change.

Despite these findings, it is important to note that the study did not look at the actual regional make-up of the member offices of INGOs, therefore avoiding asking just how international these INGOs really are. Many INGOs have grown out of Northern-based NGOs and therefore have a limited number of members from developing countries, reflecting their historical roots. What is problematic is that often many of these INGOs have numerous country offices within developing countries, but these country offices are not considered national members and are prevented from gaining access to governing and executive board decision-making processes. The weak financial muscle of developing country offices compounds this problem. INGOs that suffer from this problem should take into greater consideration how they can make their governance more international and truly representative of the places and people they purport to assist. Otherwise, they are liable to be open to criticism from the outside for not reflecting genuinely the international make-up of the organization within their governance and not learning from and listening to all their staff.

Another finding of the Trust's report was that INGOs were the least transparent sector compared with IGOs and TNCs. Many INGOs did not provide access to even basic annual reports, let alone information on more in-depth evaluation material. INGOs, in particular, stood out from the other organizations because of a lack of consistency in publishing annual reports. Three of the INGOs did not provide an annual report online: CARE International, Amnesty International (which publishes only to members) and ICFTU (which publishes a report every four years). The failure to provide this important document makes scrutiny of an INGO's finances much more difficult. Even those INGOs that do produce an annual report varied substantially in their financial disclosure. Only the IFRC made its audited account available in its annual report.

Of concern was the use of the term 'annual report' itself by some INGOs. For example, both Amnesty International and ICFTU published reports labelled as such, but both documents were largely focused on human rights abuses or trade union issues, respectively, around the world in a given year. Confusingly, they both included a section on their activities but failed to provide financial information. Regulation at the national level could address this problem partially. One idea would be for a global standard to be created that clearly indicates what should be included in a basic annual report of an INGO.

INGOs were also not good at providing evaluation material to the public. There was generally limited disclosure of evaluation material relating to their activities. Publication of evaluations is important to enable stakeholders to assess the effectiveness of INGOs' work. Much work is being undertaken by INGOs to establish guidelines that enable effective evaluation, but this is not currently published online. Only IFRC systematically provided evaluation material online. CARE, Oxfam International and WWF provide material on an ad hoc basis, but Amnesty International, the ICC and ICFTU had none at all. The last three are all advocacy NGOs and face even greater problems in assessing the effectiveness of their campaigns due to the nature of their work. However, more could be done as they must certainly undertake internal evaluations of projects.

Finally, the report also found that INGOs were not very transparent when it came to issues surrounding their governance, although it should be pointed out that none of the sectors did very well in this area. Despite the majority of INGOs putting their governing articles online, governance information varied widely. IFRC, Amnesty International and the ICC provided good descriptions of governance structures. Both Oxfam International and WWF provided only brief descriptions of key decision-making bodies, and CARE International gave no description of its governance and even failed to identify the individuals on its executive body.

As a group, INGOs make limited disclosure of documentation from their governing bodies. Only the ICFTU and IFRC disclosed such documents. They provided summaries of their governing body meetings. However, none of the INGOs provided any documents relating to their executive bodies. In the case of some INGOs, Amnesty International, for example, security issues mean that disclosure may be difficult. However, to not have any information about what decisions are being taken and by which members reveals an accountability gap that should be plugged.

Although the Trust report does not draw this conclusion, it is highly likely that the INGO sector's lack of transparency is largely a result of a lack of demand from external actors for greater disclosure. This is clearly changing, as explained earlier in this chapter. It would also be reasonable to suggest that changes will occur quite quickly in this area in the near future, as has been the case with the other sectors. This is because providing greater access to information is often one of the easiest changes an organization can make if it wants to improve its accountability. Changing governance structures, for example, would require legal reform and fundamental organizational change, while improving transparency often only means making existing information available within a new domain. The presence of the internet has also reduced the costs of making information available within the public domain. It is important to highlight, however, that providing greater access to information by itself does not enhance accountability. The quality of the information and its relevance is crucial. Limited, but highly relevant information, is far more beneficial than excessive information of no real value.

The Political Nature of NGO Accountability

Despite the report highlighting a number of interesting findings in relation to the accountability of different sectors working at the global level, it was the finding that INGOs were in many cases less transparent than IGOs and TNCs that was picked up most by the media and policy-making circles. What appeared irresistible to the outside world was the idea that the very sector that made its reputation on monitoring the accountability of other organizations had itself accountability failings or gaps. The New York Times ran an article entitled 'Holding Civil Groups Accountable' (21 July 2003), which noted that 'The WTO and the World Bank scored highly for online information disclosure, while NGO's like CARE, the World Wide Fund for Nature and the International Confederation of Free Trade Unions got much lower marks'. The WTO, subject to huge criticism by NGOs for its opaque and unrepresentative decision-making structures, shouted loudly about its relatively high ranking against other IGOs and INGOs, issuing its own press release, which sat on the front page of its media section for many weeks, 'WTO gets high marks for accountability and transparency' (11 February 2003). The press release noted that it was ranked above many NGOs, like Oxfam. The experience showed the Trust the highly political nature of NGO accountability and the need to act cautiously, given this charged environment. One of the results of the experience was that the Trust set up an informal NGO Accountability Forum for local, national and international non-governmental organizations based in the UK to understand and articulate better NGO accountability and to collectively strengthen it. The forum provides a safe space for NGOs to discuss critical opportunities and problems related to their accountability, away from those that wish to raise the issue for political point scoring.

CHALLENGES FOR THE FUTURE

The Trust's study highlighted both opportunities and dangers facing INGOs. However, it only provided a partial picture of the accountability of these organizations, given that it did not assess all aspects of their accountability. Through GAP, the Trust is currently working on developing indicators for all the dimensions in order to assess organizations against the whole model. This last section explores some of the other GAP dimensions that are likely to be highly relevant to INGOs in the near future, focusing on the need for more objective evaluations, greater engagement within the sector and the need for more robust complaints and redress mechanisms.

The lack of evaluation material in the INGO sector is extremely worrying. Also of concern is the content of INGOs evaluation reports. All too often, INGO evaluation material is largely positive, glossing over problems or failures and lacking in critical analysis. This is because there are fears within the sector that being honest and open about programme and project failings may jeopardize the ability to access funds. The concern is that greater honesty in evaluation could result in penalization by donors. This is the same argument that corporations make when they state that taking the lead in honest and objective social and environmental reporting may jeopardize their ability to retain shareholders and customers. The problem lies first with donors, who need to give more reassuring signals to INGOs that greater honesty in evaluations will not result in a withdrawal of funds. Second, it lies around collective action problems; no INGO wants to be the first organization to expose potential failings and be scrutinized. INGOs need to work collectively on this issue and move towards more frank disclosure in the future. INGOs also need to expand on their engagement practices with internal and external stakeholders, as mentioned previously. This could happen in two ways. First, there is a need to engage more beneficiaries in the advocacy work of the organization.

INGOs are particularly vulnerable to attack on this front and they need to have in place robust mechanisms to protect their right to speak on issues that affect marginalized groups. Critics, for example, argue that campaigns are being driven by what advocates and campaigners working in the international political sphere perceive to be the problem, and not what those in the developing countries actually want or need (Bello, 2003). Second, there is a need to scale up existing engagement practices from the local to the international level so that they influence all levels of decision-making within an organization (Neligan et al, 2003). Organizations are already beginning to move in this direction. Save the Children UK, for example, is undertaking a review of organizational procedure and performance with the view to strengthening its accountability to key stakeholders.

ActionAid's Accountability, Learning and Planning System (ALPS) also seeks to improve interaction between staff, poor people and partners, and to bring the concerns and needs of ActionAid's beneficiaries to the centre of decision-making.

The One World Trust has produced a set of principles that it deems vital for ensuring the process of engagement, being worthwhile for both the organization and its stakeholders. These are: access to timely and accurate information; clear terms of engagement (that is, the parameters of what is subject to negotiation and what is not, clearly defined and understood); legitimate engagement procedures for selecting and working with stakeholders; and robust procedures for redress.

Presently, very few mechanisms exist for stakeholders to voice their complaints within the sector. Complaints procedures for both internal and external stakeholders are of vital importance, ensuring that organizations gain an accurate picture of the impact of their work and are able to respond quickly to grievances and problems (De Las Casas, 2005).

It is also a vital means through which to give power to stakeholders, giving them a unique opportunity to set the agenda and voice their concerns. The Humanitarian Accountability Project International (HAP-I), for example, has set up a Standing Complaints Committee for its members to deal with complaints by disaster-affected populations within the humanitarian sector. Another example is Save the Children UK's feedback committees in Zimbabwe. This involved establishing children feedback committees as a channel of communication independent from the agency to enable complaints from children, who were key beneficiaries of the projects, but whose views were previously little heard, to make complaints and have them responded to (McIvor, 2004).

INGOs should work in collaboration on this issue, looking, perhaps, into an ombudsman for the sector that could be applicable to all types of INGOs, or developing different ombudsmen for different types of INGOs. The most important challenge facing INGOs in the future is the need for a more pro-active approach to the accountability issue by the sector itself. It is no longer tenable for an INGO to claim that their accountability rests on moral authority alone. Today, INGOs are required to be accountable to a wide number of stakeholders: trustees, staff, donors, governments and, most importantly, to their beneficiaries-the individuals and communities they serve.

Calls for greater transparency, more constructive measurement and evaluation of NGO programmes and clearer and more robust governance structures are increasingly heard. These demands need to be viewed positively. They provide a welcome opportunity for the sector to not only strengthen its own internal learning mechanisms and to become more efficient and effective, but also to enhance and embed the legitimacy and standing of INGOs within society.

INGOs need to start taking the issue seriously and they need to work collaboratively to define the agenda and avoid having it shaped by those outside of the sector. Defensive posturing or putting one's head in the sand can be a disaster. As John Elkington notes citing the corporate sector's experience: Shell, in 1995 was totally taken by surprise by what happened to them (Brent Spa), as was Anderson. People don't see stuff coming and I think it's the same with NGOs. There's a very real risk that one or more NGOs will be caught up in an accountability issue... But when the issue comes, the spikes come very, very fast, and the reaction time allowed by the media for companies or NGOs are [sic] precariously short. (Jepson, 2004)

The corporations and intergovernmental organizations that have been successful in this area are those that have faced the challenge proactively, admitted weakness and mistakes and have in an open and transparent manner tried to rectify them. INGOs need to learn from the experience of other sectors and take action before an Enron-style scandal forces them to take it. It is vital that the accountability mechanisms adopted by the INGO sector enhance rather than detract from the sector's work. It is crucial that the mechanisms adopted by INGOs contribute towards their dynamic and often fluid nature and add to their ability to be important critical voices on issues around the world. 'The challenge is to identify mechanisms that promote rights and accountability, by seeking ways to articulate NGO responsibilities that do not endanger the political space for the many positive roles that NGOs can play in securing rights' (Jordan, 2004). All global organizations are facing questions regarding their accountability. This is part of a re-questioning by society of the rights, roles and responsibilities of all institutions in the light of globalization. INGOs have been drawn into this debate, and given their extremely important role within the world it is vital they take up this challenge.

BRIDGING THE NGO-BANKER DIVIDE

The role of non-governmental organisations (NGOs) in microfinance (mF) needs reviewing from an operational perspective. Based on research of selective studies and experts' opinion, selected literature on microfinance, and the author's own experience over the last decade, this paper seeks to establish two main points. First, it asserts that with a few notable exceptions, the record of NGOs in mainstreaming microfinance is a modest one viewed from the context of NGOs as microfinance institutions (mFIs). When judged by the two criteria of success that much of the microfinance world has adopted – outreach to the poor and financial sustainability – the results are not encouraging [Nair 2001]. NGOs as mFIs have thus far had trouble achieving both objectives simultaneously. There is also little evidence of any aggregate impact on poverty reduction as the result of mFIs' forays. The success of NGOs has however been laudable where facilitating and social intermediation criteria are applied. It is here that the author feels that the strategic partnership between banks and NGOs is poised to change the developmental intervention map of India. Second, the essay suggests that banks, for all their laudable work, will be making a strategic error in focusing on financial intermediation while ignoring partnership with NGOs. While microfinance is never easy for other types of institutions trying to practise it (e g, NGOs or credit unions), it is not, as will be explained, a field where a banker has natural advantages.

To the extent that banks incorporate NGOs' activities in mainstreaming their self-help group (SHG) portfolios, they stand to gain. To the extent NGOs reorient their mission, vision and personnel towards the microfinance agenda, as a large number have done in the last decade, they risk drawing themselves away from work they are uniquely suited to do. Some of this work, moreover, would play a critical role in preparing the ground for mF among poor people. In other words, NGOs have to move away from pure financial intermediation to investing in human and social capital at the grass roots and bankers have to tap this invaluable experience of NGOs in mobilising, graduating and enabling rural communities. This will prepare the ground by enhancing credit absorption capacity of SHGs and enhancing their creditworthiness. The following account will explain how.

In 1997, the World Bank's Sustainable Banking for the Poor (SBP) project completed an ambitious survey. Until then those interested in microfinance had an intuitive sense of the movement's growth, but no systematic attempt had yet been made to gauge its dimensions, nor look comprehensively at its results. The findings were unambiguous: NGOs acting as mFIs did not have any significant outreach vis-à-vis other financial institutions purveying microcredit.

Interestingly, commercial banks accounted for 78 per cent of the total number of outstanding microloans, and credit unions 11 per cent. NGOs accounted for only 9 per cent, and savings banks (which are not primarily in the credit business) just 2 per cent. Also, commercial banks accounted for 68 per cent of the total outstanding loan balance, savings banks 15 per cent, credit unions 13 per cent and NGOs 4 per cent.

In terms of numbers of clients, commercial banks and credit unions showed significantly greater overall outreach than NGOs. While NGOs' outreach, on average, was deeper, it was also narrow – NGOs reach some very poor people, but they do not reach many. On the other hand, credit unions and commercial banks also serve some wealthier clients so that their average outreach to the poor is not as deep. Still, the indications are that overall, credit unions and commercial banks serve more under-served poor clients than do NGOs.

This is not to rule out the role of NBFCs, NGOs with inchoate mFI activities or pure mFIs. The demand for financial services is high and as stated by the High Level Task Force on mF: "At least 25,000 bank branches, 4,000 NGOs and 2,000 federations of SHGs involving over 1,00,000 personnel of these institutions would have to be associated for scaling up and bank linkage of one million SHGs. Many of these NGOs will transform themselves into mFIs and will not only facilitate microfinancing, but will also themselves do the necessary financial intermediation. Similarly, many federations of SHGs will take on financial intermediation and act as mFIs."

Indian Tale

We shift the focus to India.In the current context with over 4,60,000 SHGs credit-linked with banks, the SHG-bank linkage programme of microfinance has emerged as the biggest in the world. But besides banks, the major role played by NGOs in facilitating this transformation cannot be overemphasised.

The National Bank for Agriculture and Rural Development (NABARD) which plays a role in promoting and facilitating bank linkages while networking and coordinating the activities of all players in the field has underscored the crucial role played by NGOs as facilitators in purveying bank credit to SHGs. The story of the three models of this massive programme has been brought out by NABARD in the table.

The writing is on the wall. The success story has been to a great extent co-scripted by both banks and NGOs. However, it is pertinent to draw attention here to the vast network of rural banking outlets that precludes the necessity of a new breed of mFIs which as per experts' opinion are 'slow and expensive to develop' [Harper 2002]. In fact as aptly put by Harper "the SHG system uses existing marketing channels, the banks, to bring formal financial services to a new market segment, the poor and particularly women".

COMPETITIVE ADVANTAGE OF NGOS

NGOs have a crucial role in group formation, nurturing SHGs in the pre-microenterprise stage, capacity building and enhancing credit absorption capacities. Group-based forms of lending (e g, solidarity groups, village banking) originated mainly for the benefit of the lender as solutions to two problems faced by microcredit organisations: (i) the problem of lack of collateral, and (ii) the problem of high transaction costs involved in loan appraisal, monitoring and enforcement.

In theory, the group serves as a set of co-guarantors operating through peer pressure and the group members' incentive to keep each other solvent so that they themselves do not lose the opportunity to receive a loan. The group serves also as a way to get around imperfect information, since members of the group know each other. Thus the transaction costs involved in loan appraisal are reduced if not eliminated.

It is here that NGOs play the crucial role in transforming the atypical destitute village woman with two children to fend for into a responsible individual with group commitments and group resources. This is a fact repeated in village after village. Whether NGOs empower women in thrift and credit groups is a moot question but it is an empirical fact that such groups provide effective 'coping mechanisms'. Peer pressure is the best collateral. The banker in India needs to recognise that high repayment rates of SHGs is not an inherent structural feature of SHGs but a commitment to group values. The role of NGOs in investing groups with values through human capital is an undeniable specialisation.

In the words of economist Jagdish Bhagwati: "Those values (of civil society and of democracy) are better advanced...by the political and financial support of the numerous and growing NGOs, both here and abroad, that work ceaselessly to nudge the world in the right direction."

The term social intermediation is meant to suggest that there is another kind of intermediation (other than financial) that institutions can engage in which also supports microfinance. Social intermediation implicitly acknowledges that many poor clients of microfinance are simply not in a position to use loans productively. Social intermediation refers to a range of activities that prepares people to become good borrowers and savers, better manage their own finances or their own financial groups and help them to put whatever 'social capital' they have to more productive use.

Because social intermediation activities imply interacting closely with people at the grass roots, these activities are a good fit with the classic characteristics of NGOs. The trade-off, of course, is that such interventions are not likely to be financially self-sustainable. They need instead to be seen as human capital investments.

The banker must accept that this is a role which the NGO, as a committed social engineer, is better suited to execute. This is not to deny qualities of empathy, humanism, social engineering to bankers. But the stark truth is that there is a need for a sensible division of labour. If bankers want to reach the poorest with financial services, they need to face certain realities. First, what they are doing is poverty lending and not economic development or enterprise development. Second, they should realise what the likely impacts may be. Changes in people's lives will be immediate in terms of lightening the burdens of poverty, but small loans to the poorest will not bring them permanently out of poverty.

Social engineering is a full-time activity which has no substitute for the limited community contacts that a committed banker might indulge in. Moreover, the calling of retail banking has its own demands while credit plus initiatives are the forte of NGOs. Similarly, the NGO's salvation lies in channelising formal credit to his clientele through innovations so as to meet the overall needs of socio-economic empowerment. The banker's goal is to secure loans through credit plus interventions which improve creditworthiness of SHGs. But certainly NGOs are positioned at the community level to educate and prepare local institutions and people to be able to make more effective use of the opportunities and better use of finance.

The business of a rural branch can move from sustainability to high profits when SHGs make the important shift from pre-microenterprise stage to microenterprise stage but a lot of social and technical inputs from outside the quintessential rural SHG are required for this.

Small businesses (and dynamic micro-enterprises) need to develop skills. NGOs can assist by creating institutions to train and teach, or work with existing institutions to make what they teach more relevant to the clients. Small businesses (and dynamic micro-enterprises) need to develop the capacity to become and remain competitive. NGOs with good community organising skills can work to get businesses to pool resources within a sub-sector to develop new products, new product designs, or new techniques for production that maximise local resources. Policy level constraints at the sub-sector level can be identified by NGOs who know the local market terrain, and NGOs can bring these issues to the policy-making table.

Arguably, banking is more of a system than an art. Unarguably, working to facilitate the productivity of small businesses is really an art. And again, because of their grass roots orientation, because of their commitment, because they are less bureaucratic and encumbered than large development assistance organisations, NGOs are capable of overcoming a subtle but important barrier to successful facilitation – the 'packaging of knowledge and skills'.

Once again, this is no case for discouraging NGOs from mF but to emphasise the role of emotional capital which will bring in an element of quality. The more NGOs, who are in microfinance, face the challenge of helping to bring about an increased articulation of the parts and the players in a local economy, the more they may need to get involved in such non-financial services. The effects of such services are difficult to measure in the short run. But NGOs can take on such tasks, many already do so.

Thus, NGOs will fill up an important void in quality at the grass roots level which will help the poor not only to borrow but also to become good investments for banks. This will help boost business at rural branch level and cover up inadequacies and constraints that might hamper a banker with the conflicting demands of his workload. Many banks and FIs have recognised the role of NGOs and have effected suitable policy initiatives. A larger recognition of this need is reflected in the statistical evidence on linkage patterns, which we have cited earlier, which establishes NGO-bank partnership over the Indian mF spectrum.

A truer recognition at individual banker level might lead to business sense replacing customary scepticism for NGOs. This will be the strategic turning point in making India's relationship banking a showpiece and paradigm for the world's NGOs and bankers.

Bibliography

- Anderson, Mary : *Managing Global Chaos: Sources of and Responses to International Conflict,* Washington, DC: United States Institute of Peace Press, 1996.
- Arruda, Marcos : *NGOs and the World Bank: Is It Possible to Collaborate Critically?,* Rio de Janeiro: PACS, 1995.
- Carroll, Thomas : *Intermediary NGOs: the supporting link in grassroots development,* West Hartford, CT: Kumarian Press, 1992.
- David Brown: *The Struggle for Accountability: The World Bank, NGOs, and Grassroots Movements,* Cambridge, Mass.: MIT Press, 1998.
- David Hulme: *Beyond the Magic Bullet: NGO performance and accountability in the post-cold war world,* West Hartford, Kumarian Press, 1996.
- Florini, M. : *The Third Force: The Rise of Transnational Civil Society,* Washington, DC: Carnegie Endowment for International Peace, 2000.
- Harold K. Jacobson: *Networks of Interdependence: international organizations and the global political system,* New York, Knopf, 1984.
- John Boli and George Thomas: *Constructing World Culture: International Nongovernmental*

Organizations Since 1875, Stanford, Stanford University Press, 1999.

- John Ehrenberg: *Civil Society: The Critical History of an Idea,* New York, New York University Press, 1998.
- Kees Biekart: *The Politics of Civil Society Building: European Private Aid Agencies and Democratic Transitions in Central America,* Utrecht, International Books, 1999.
- Leon Gordenker: *NGOs, the UN & Global Governance,* Boulder, Lynne Riener, 1996.
- Matthias Finger: *Environmental NGOs in World Politics,* London, Routledge, 1994.
- Nelson, J. : *The World Bank and NGOs: The Limits of Apolitical Development,* New York, St. Martin's Press, 1995.
- Paul Wapner: *Environmental Activism and World Civic Politics,* Albany, SUNY Press, 1996.
- Pentikaiine, Antti n: *Creating Global Governance - The Role of Non-Governmental Organizations in the United Nations,* Helsinki, Finnish UN Association 2000.
- Peter Willetts: *Pressure Groups in the Global System,* London, Francis Pinter, 1982
- Sarah Burns: *Movers and Shapers: NGOs in International Affairs,* Washington DC, World Resources Institute, 1994.

Index

H

I

L

M

N

O

P

R

S

□□□